FOR MEN ONLY

A GENTLEMAN'S GUIDE TO GREAT ENTERTAINING

NAOMI TORRE POULSON

AINSLIE STREET PRESS

MONARCH BEACH, CALIFORNIA

© 2006 by Naomi Torre Poulson. All rights reserved.

No part of this publication may be reproduced, distributed, or transmitted in any form or by any means, including photocopying, recording, or other electronic or mechanical methods, or by any information storage and retrieval system, without prior written permission from the publisher, except for brief quotations embodied in critical reviews and certain other noncommercial uses permitted by copyright law. For permission requests, write to the publisher, at the address below.

Ainslie Street Press
P.O. Box 25689
Santa Ana, CA 92799
(800) 354-5348
Attention: Permissions Coordinator

Individual Sales. This book is available through most bookstores or can be ordered directly from Seven Locks Press at the address above.

Quantity Sales. Special discounts are available on quantity purchases by corporations, associations, and others. For details, contact the "Special Sales Department" at the publisher's address above.

Printed in the United States of America

Library of Congress Cataloging-in-Publication Data
is available from the publisher
ISBN 0-9762885-1-6

Cover and interior design by Heather Buchman
Illustrations by Avery Ota

The author and publisher assume neither liability nor responsibility to any person or entity with respect to any direct or indirect loss or damage caused, or alleged to be caused, by the information contained herein, or for errors, omissions, inaccuracies, or any other inconsistency within these pages, or for unintentional slights against people or organizations.

To my beloved husband,
for supporting me in (almost)
everything I do.

CONTENTS

Foreword		vii
Preface		xi
Acknowledgments		xv
Introduction		xvii
Chapter 1	The Singles Scene	1
Chapter 2	Hosting a Social Dinner at Home	28
Chapter 3	How to Dine	59
Chapter 4	Entertaining for Business	86
Chapter 5	All You Need to Know About Wine (for Now)	96
Chapter 6	The Order of Wine Service	104
Chapter 7	Bottles, Corkscrews, Pouring, and More	117
Appendix A	Food and Wine Pairing	137
Appendix B	Cheese, Fruit, Chocolate, and Dessert	155
Appendix C	Index of Wine and Spirit Terms	159
Appendix D	Wine and Spirit Pronunciation Guide	163
Appendix E	Menu Guide	168
Appendix F	Tipping Guide	182
Bibliography		188
Index		189
Professional Profile		196

FOREWORD

Enjoying is the Best Way
CARLETON VARNEY

Not every man can look like Cary Grant or talk like Maurice Chevalier or Louis Jordan. And not every man has the savoir faire of Franchot Tone or Charles Boyer. Oh, how sad that today there are no male stars who can truly be called matinee idols. This isn't the day of the man in the gray and white double-breasted suit with polished shoes, buffed nails and a great haircut. Today's man is a guy with a shaved head (God love Yul Brynner) and with hip-hugging or sagging jeans. He dates long-legged babes with bellybuttons showing, taking them to the theater and to fancy—or are they?—nightclubs. There are places, such as George Club and Harry's Bar in London, where a man still pulls out a chair for a lady or offers her a smile when she looks demurely at the dinner menu.

What about the restaurant owner who instructs the waiter to tell the cost of each and every appetizer and entrée, after reciting them? A man who entertains knows well—or should know well—the prices at the restaurants he frequents.

Or should a man always pick up the tab? In the olden days, the man paid while the lady drank champagne. Gone are the days of screen idols and the days when male entertaining meant the man always pays.

Since I have never been a guy who didn't pay the bill for my dates, wife, or family or friends, I guess I would be called old-fashioned.

Entertaining friends at dinner, or at the theater, is always a pleasurable experience for me—and quite honestly—I enjoy the company, and I'm happy to pay for the pleasure I receive. When I invite a guest or two or three or four, I invite them for their company. The only thing I ever ask of my guests is that they extend to my other guests their conversation, wit and graciousness. A party that works occurs only when each guest accepts a responsibility. The responsibility is to help make an evening of entertaining fun for everyone invited.

The man of today who loves to entertain has to know, and care, about the "whens," the "how tos" and the "how nots" of what to wear at a function, how to get there, how to order, how much to drink, and, in general, how to behave.

Entertaining is different from one function to another. A picnic luncheon from the back of a station wagon is different than dining on caviar and champagne at the Dublin Embassy with Ambassador and Mrs. Egan. And a smart man is he who knows how to wear tweeds and corduroys at the races.

Entertaining, believe it or not, and being entertained, believe it or not, have to be fun. If it isn't going to be fun, stay home and hop into bed with a cup of hot milk.

Those guys who want to have fun will enjoy this book.

PREFACE

When Naomi asked me to preface her book on entertaining, I was delighted. I have spent the last few years encouraging an international market back into entertaining at home, and wish Naomi every success in her endeavour to show people just how easy it is for the modern man to entertain, compared to twenty or thirty years ago.

We live in an age of gourmet delicatessens, delicious ready-made dishes, easy access to fine-wine cellars, and fabulous flowers and decorative inspiration. However, manners maketh man, and it is impossible to give your guests a wonderful evening if you do not have the confidence and social skills to carry off the perfect food and wine. Women want as much control in the boardroom as do the chaps, but show me a lady who does not secretly want doors to be held open for her, who is not thrilled when you collect her for a date, or when you offer to order for her in a restaurant.

What is the key to successful entertaining? I believe it is very simple: a relaxed and inviting atmosphere, good company, good food and good wine, underpinned by impeccable social skills.

In a fast-paced world, corporate professionals have only seconds to make favourable first impressions, and our manners and social skills are under constant scrutiny. Because of this, we all need to have perfected interpersonal skills as well as technical ones that are required for our professions; we must be ready for and able to adapt to change, perhaps in situations where we are meeting or entertaining visitors from overseas.

For those executives expected to entertain socially, or professional colleagues for the first time, relax! Cultivate the skills of introductions, set an inviting table, and invite your guests according to the nature of the event. Match similar interests or professions as well as humour and charisma. For a first occasion, keep it small. It is much easier to cook for six than it is for twelve, and practice really does make perfect. Entertaining, whether on a budget or grand formal scale, will be more enjoyable the more planning that goes into it.

For entertaining at home:
- Decide what type of event you wish to hold, seated or standing, large or small, formal or informal.
- Cook ahead and make use of your freezer and neighbourhood delicatessens. Try to select recipes that are quick, which keep well or which can be prepared or partly

prepared in advance, and balance your choices in color and texture as much as possible.
- Have a good mix of guests—give careful thought to your invitation list.
- Set a budget and use it to create a good ambience, with candles, flowers and décor. Match napkins and table linen or at least colour-coordinate your theme.
- Ensure you know any special dietary requirements for your guests.
- Choose your menu carefully and make sure you give thought to the drinks.

— Alexandra Messervy
Formerly of the household of
Her Majesty the Queen

ACKNOWLEDGMENTS

I wish to thank the following people who supported me throughout the writing of this book.

John Chaffetz for his encouragement and who gave time and advice at the early stages of this endeavor; Dom Zeim, Brian Cronin, James Drakeford, and Thomas Curran for their expert conributions to the food and wine sections, Dorothea Johnson who shared her knowledge and became a friend, Alexandra Messervy and Carleton Varney for not hesitating to contribute to the project.

From Seven Locks Press I wish to thank Kira Fulks who saw the potential of *For Men Only*; Jim Riordan for his patience; Barbara Chuck, who edited the manuscript; Heather Buchman for revising and re-revising the layout; and Avery Ota for the illustrations.

INTRODUCTION

The whole point about prestige is that it is possessed by few—what is available to the multitudes is devalued by the very fact of being "common."

—Margaret Visser

Is it my imagination, or are most books and magazine articles written for men telling them how to win over women, written by men? Well, I've been a woman for a long time, and I *know* what a level-headed, sophisticated woman finds really sexy in a man, and it's much more full of depth than his biceps. Good looks and a fabulous body may be a great entrée to a lot of shallow females, but personally, I've always preferred a man who kissed *me* in the morning, not his mirror. A sophisticated woman wants her man to be a good provider, talented, powerful, and cultured. In short, she wants a man who reflects her good taste. When the first blush of romantic ecstasy is over, it's a man's basic qualities of intellect, knowledge and generosity that carry the day.

There are two ways to become these things. You can be to the manor born, or you can develop these qualities in yourself. For most of us, it's the latter. If that's your case also, you'll just have to work harder. In the old Hollywood studio stables, hopeful men and women were put through their paces: They learned deportment, elocution, and how to dress, speak correctly, drop their regional accents, and even walk. In essence, they learned to have star quality. Self-made men reinvent themselves. Why not you?

People are impressed by those who know how to present themselves well. If you want to acquire recognition from your friends and/or business associates, you will set yourself apart by knowing how to dance and how to carve a turkey. Too bad these opportunities don't pop up very often. However, everyone eats and drinks. Knowing how to entertain with panache is a skill that almost always garners admiration.

One of the ways a man can do this is to know his way around restaurants, food and wine. What can be more sensual than wining and dining a woman in style? After reading *For Men Only—A Gentleman's Guide to Great Entertaining*, you will know how to entertain like a pro and how to navigate your way around an array of wines, whether at a picnic or at a seven-course dinner.

This book is an introduction into changing your self-image, self-esteem, self-confidence, yourself. Want it. Taste it. Feel it. Live it.

CHAPTER 1
THE SINGLES SCENE

Image is everything.

—André Agassi

You say you want to meet a 10. Think. Does a 10 want to meet *you*? Have you ever seen the movie classic *Marty*, starring Ernest Borgnine? It's the story of a pudgy, working-class man who eventually takes an honest look at himself while being chided by his pedestrian friends for dating a shy, ordinary woman. The message is: Like attracts like. Don't be hesitant to ask any woman out. Plain Jane may turn out to be your soul mate and a person of depth. Miss America may be sitting at home because everyone else has found her to be too intimidating or too high maintenance.

It may seem strange, but a dinner for two people can be more daunting than a party for six or more. Why? Because for a large group of people, after you provide the food, drink, and music, guests manage to amuse themselves. When it is just you and a woman, you are definitely on display. But there is no real need to feel dismayed, because you have already practiced entertaining when you've taken a client to lunch, had dinner with a colleague, and had dress rehearsals with your friends and relatives. You're not a neophyte anymore. You've learned how to set a table, time your dinner, choose wines, and direct conversation; you know that when you invite a woman to your home for a candlelit dinner, until you find out the lady's preference, you either put your pet in another section of the house or leave your dog or cat with a neighbor. The rules are the same for every experience: You plan, take care of the details, show creativity and caring. Besides, most women won't be expecting an extravagant feast. Smart women are impressed by a man who possesses social savvy. The fact that you can entertain at all is astonishing to them. So, if you want to win over a 10, you have to be one as well. You do want a woman with class, don't you?

DECOR

The appeal of your home is just as important as the food and wine you serve. Don't neglect how you live. Set the stage. **Make sure your home is absolutely spotless.** Years ago I read in a men's magazine that a man's bachelor quarters are clean, organized, and well-appointed. It's a boy (no matter how old) who is simply living away from Mom who takes no pride in his surroundings. Women of quality are not impressed by a pigsty house. A dirty, sticky house is the biggest turnoff I can think of. If you wish to entertain a woman in your home, you must live like an adult, not a teenager on the loose. Kitchens and bathrooms are sparkling, clothing is put away, furniture is dusted, towels and linens are freshly laundered, toilet bowl lids are down, toothpaste caps are replaced—the works. Make this a lifestyle, not an artificial, one-time effort to fool the lady. It won't work for long.

AMBIENCE

Avoid turning on harsh, overhead lighting, which makes people look ghostly. Instead use lamp lighting, and, better still, candles. Candlelight is not only romantic, but also women know they look better in it, and this puts them in a convivial mood. Place candles in groups of three or five on the table as part of your centerpiece and about your home.

MUSIC

You've ditched your trucker caps, traded in your sweat shirts and plaid shorts for business clothing, and now rock music from hell no longer has a place in your heart—not if you want to upgrade your image and take your place in the world as an adult. Background music should be just that—in the background, mellow, unobtrusive, and conducive to conversation.

A ROMANTIC DINNER FOR TWO

When I worked at the Jet Propulsion Laboratory in La Cañada-Flintridge, California, the computer engineers used the acronym KISS (Keep It Simple, Stupid). The following menus for two are from traditional recipes that have six or fewer ingredients. There is little preparation time. She'll think you are marvelous.

A word of caution: **All your ingredients must be fresh and of the highest quality**. Find out on which days your specialty stores get their deliveries of fresh produce. Invest in a pepper mill. Preground pepper won't do.

Choose which courses you'd like to serve from the following possibilities:

Dinner # 1

Prosciutto e fichi (Italian cured ham with figs)
Stracciatella (egg-drop soup)
Salmon Steak
Patate alla Trattoria–Trattoria Baked Potatoes
Caprese–Tomato and Mozzarella Salad
Crunchy Italian Bread
Fried Bananas Flambé and Fresh Coffee
Bardolino Wine

Prosciutto e fichi (Italian cured ham with figs)

- 5 ounces Prosciutto de Parma (the real deal), very thinly sliced. Have your deli slice it for you.
- 8 fully ripe figs (thinly sliced and seeded pieces of cantaloupe may be substituted)
- Pepper to taste

1. Place the figs in the refrigerator to cool.
2. Spread the prosciutto on a serving dish.
3. Quarter the figs lengthwise.
4. Wrap the figs in slices of prosciutto.
5. Secure with a toothpick, sprinkle with pepper, and serve.

Crackers or bread may accompany this dish.

Stracciatella (egg-drop soup)

- 4 cups chicken or vegetable broth
- 4 eggs
- 4 tablespoons of freshly grated Parmesan-Reggiano cheese. (Accept no substitute and don't buy it in a box.)
- 1 tablespoon all-purpose flour
- Salt and pepper to taste

1. Heat the broth until hot.

2. In a bowl, mix eggs until fluffy. Add the cheese, flour, and salt and pepper.
3. Slowly whisk the mixture into the hot broth. Stir the soup in a circular motion to create a whirlpool. Drizzle the egg mixture into the sides of the liquid.
4. Cook over low heat 4–5 minutes, whisking constantly to form small, shredded pieces of egg.

Broiled Salmon Steaks

¾	pound wild salmon steaks, preferably without skin
¼	cup olive oil
2	tablespoons light soy sauce
1	tablespoon freshly snipped dill or a dash dried dill weed
	Juice of a small lemon
	Dash ground clove

1. Pre-heat oven to 425°. Place steaks in a baking dish.
2. Mix the next five ingredients together well and pour over the salmon.
3. Broil steaks on both sides until tender, about 10–12 minutes. When knife is inserted, the flesh should be opaque. Do not overcook.
4. Sprinkle with dill and serve.

Patate alla Trattoria–Trattoria Baked Potatoes

> 2 Russet potatoes
> 1 small yellow onion, peeled and chopped
> 1/4 cup olive oil
> 1 tablespoon flour
> Salt and pepper to taste
> Lemon juice (optional)

1. Peel, rinse in cold water, and dice potatoes into 1/2-inch cubes. Parboil in hot water for 5 minutes.
2. Mix next 4 ingredients in a large bowl. Add potatoes and mix again. Arrange in a buttered baking dish.
3. Bake at 400° until fork comes out easily, about 30–35 minutes.
4. Pour lemon juice over potatoes and serve hot.

Caprese–Tomato and Mozzarella Salad

> 1 large tomato, sliced
> 2 small balls of fresh mozzarella, sliced
> 1/4 pound Italian or Greek olives
> 1 tablespoon of olive oil or bottled Italian dressing
> Salt and freshly ground pepper
> Basil

1. Rinse the tomatoes, remove the stem portion, and cut them into slices.

2. Slice the mozzarella balls ¼-inch thick.
3. Arrange the tomato and mozzarella into alternate slices on a serving plate. Season with salt and fresh pepper.
4. Intersperse the olives on the plate.
5. Pour olive oil or Italian dressing over, and decorate with washed, trimmed basil leaves.

Fried Bananas Flambé

- 1½ tablespoons butter
- 2 large medium-ripe bananas, peeled
- 1 tablespoon sugar
- ¼ cup rum, warmed in a small saucepan over low heat until it almost simmers.

1. Melt butter in a small skillet.
2. Roll the bananas in the butter.
3. Sprinkle with the sugar and fry in butter until tender, about 1–2 minutes.
4. Remove bananas from skillet and pour warmed rum over bananas.
5. Ignite.

Dinner # 2

Chilled Strawberry Soup
Filet Mignon

Pasta with Herb Butter
Crunchy French Bread
Cabernet Sauvignon
Chocolate Mousse

Chilled Strawberry Soup

- 1 pint rinsed and hulled strawberries
- 1 pint buttermilk
- 1/4 cup sugar
- 1/4 cup sour cream
- 2 tablespoons kirsch (cherry liqueur)

1. Blend ingredients in a blender or food processor. Serve chilled.

Filet Mignon

- 2 filets mignon
- Onion salt and pepper to taste
- Kitchen Bouquet™ sauce

1. Baste the filets with onion salt and pepper and Kitchen Bouquet™ sauce.
2. Puncture the meat with a fork several times so it absorbs the flavoring.
3. Place meat on a rack over a pan to catch dripping, and broil until desired doneness.

Pasta

- 2 quarts of water
- ½ pound of pasta
- 1 tablespoon salt

1. Start with cold water and bring it to a boil. Add the salt. Add the pasta **all at once** when the salted water has come to a rolling boil. Never break long spaghetti in half. Bend it in the middle with a wooden spoon to push it all under water.
2. Stir with a wooden spoon to keep it from sticking together. Cover the pot to hasten cooking time, but watch it closely so that the water doesn't spill over.
3. When the water returns to a boil, uncover, and cook rapidly until it is *al dente*, or "firm to the tooth." Pasta should never be cooked until it's limp. Ignore the time directions on the box, since heat source, hardness of water, and manufacturer all have a bearing on doneness. You'll have to pick out a strand with a fork and taste it.
4. As soon as the pasta is done, stop the cooking and drain it immediately. Use a colander. Shake it about to drain out all the water. Transfer to a warmed serving bowl. I like to drain out the hot water into a bowl to warm it, and then empty it before adding the pasta. Or place the bowl in a toaster oven, if you have one, to warm it.

5. Add the herb butter, toss, and serve immediately so that the pasta doesn't continue to soften or get cold.

Herb Butter

- ½ cup butter, softened
- Any combination of 1 tablespoon of chopped fresh parsley, oregano, chives, savory, basil, thyme, or rosemary

1. Combine butter and herbs thoroughly.
2. Melt and pour over pasta, or allow to set for 30 minutes and spread over bread.

Chocolate Mousse

- 3 ounces semisweet chocolate
- 1½ tablespoons hot espresso coffee
- 1 egg
- ½ cup scalded milk
- 1 tablespoon Kahlúa

1. To scald milk, place it in a heavy-bottomed pot. Heat the milk over medium heat until a thin film is produced on top of the milk and a few bubbles just break through; once hot, remove the pot from the burner.

2. Combine ingredients in a food processor or blender and process for 2 minutes.
3. Pour mixture into compotes or wineglasses.
4. Chill 3–4 hours.
5. Serve topped with whipped cream and chocolate shavings, fresh raspberries, or mint sprigs (optional).

Odd Stuff

- Quality food is the hallmark of quality people. Avoid shopping for your food at your local chain supermarket. Seek out specialty stores for that incredible home-made bread, imported olives, and desserts or cheeses.

- Pasta as a separate course is eaten from a large, rounded dish, not a flat plate. I like angel hair, penne, and bow ties. Of course, fresh pasta is best, but for those who are minus a pasta making machine or in a rush, you can buy freshly packaged pasta in most markets, in the deli department. If you buy dry pasta, get a brand made in Italy. Italy has superior-quality products to those made in the States.

- Do not use iceberg lettuce when making a green salad. Make a salad from butter and/or romaine lettuce. Add any combination of endive, arugula, watercress, radicchio, and young spinach. Or, you can get fresh prewashed and premixed salad in a bag from your grocer. Add your own additional fixings. Calculate a handful of salad per person.

- If you serve instant coffee, you'll be toast. Buy Colombian or Kona beans.

- Purchase a coffee grinder. For convenience, keep the coffee canister next to it on the kitchen counter. It takes less than fifteen seconds to grind two tablespoons of coffee.

- Purchase a French press coffee maker. It takes another few seconds to pour the ground coffee and the water into it, and to press down the plunger.

- Candles are not lit during the day.

ENTERTAINING A WOMAN IN A RESTAURANT

The two things that woman have complained the loudest to me about men are: 1. Their male friends don't like to dress up, and 2. Many men don't know how to eat. There is no excuse for scoffing food into your mouth (with or without a fork), talking with your mouth open, and smacking like a hog, hunching over your food, pawing your utensils, and dripping sauce down your chin. Get the picture? Knuckle draggers are an embarrassment to quality women.

You can learn good table manners by looking at old movies, and current movies set in the 1950s and earlier. Open your eyes, watch what others do. Question people whom you admire; ask them to tell you what you're doing wrong. There is an entirely different set of rules for social and business entertainment. Both men and women must be able to make the switch after leaving the office world behind them. Savvy women who are dynamos in the boardroom morph into feminine women in the bedroom. You rise to the occasion when you attend to that softer side of her by being comfortable opening car doors, standing up when she comes to the dinner table, pulling out her chair, and eating in a manner that says culture and breeding.

The Rules of Engagement

- Don't ask out a woman fewer than three days in advance; it suggests that she is an afterthought or, worse, your second or maybe your third pick. No female wants to be thought of as sitting around, waiting for Prince Charming to rescue her from a life of stultifying dullness. A smart, self-confident woman will turn you down rather than accept a last-minute invitation. Never ask, "Are you free next Friday night?" The answer inevitably will be "No." A less pedestrian request is, "I was wondering if you would like to have dinner [see a play] with me sometime soon?" If there is a genuine reason for a turndown, such as "I'd very much like to, but I have a prior engagement," the lady will probably tack on, "Perhaps we can make it another evening?" When you ask out a woman, and she states that she's busy for the next three months, it means she doesn't want to date you, for whatever reason. Don't keep asking, and don't take it personally. You're not attracted to every woman you meet, either.

- Judith Martin, better known by her pen name "Miss Manners," says there should be three parts to a date, of which at least two must be offered: entertainment, food, and affection. At first, a gentleman places the greatest weight on the entertainment, secondly on the food, and only a hint on affection. After several dates, the affection may become the entertainment, but the food must never be omitted.

- If you don't know the woman well, keep your first date casual. As in any transaction between people, rapport needs to be built before it can go forward. A good choice would be someplace where you can fill the time discussing the event—a film or art festival, a museum, play, or concert. Invite her somewhere you think she would enjoy. Taking a classical music lover to a professional wrestling match isn't good planning!

- If the first date is going to revolve around food, dinner is not a good choice since it is more suggestive. Lunch or after-work drinks are more casual. Avoid a restaurant that is noisy, too extravagant, or too private. Ask her what kind of food she likes.

- **Call the day before to confirm the arrangements.** This not only shows that you are indeed going to show up, it allows her to clear her calendar in the event of a misunderstanding. If you haven't already, you can tell her where you are going, so that she can dress appropriately, and what time you will come to collect her.

- The only thank you a woman owes a man in exchange for accepting a date with him is her company. Expect nothing else. A woman may offer to go Dutch as a signal that she has accepted the date out of politeness only, and has no intention of going forward with the relationship.

Make the Reservation

Don't assume that there will be a table waiting for you when you arrive at a restaurant. You will look inept if you arrive at an establishment and have to be turned away because you didn't plan ahead. For an upscale restaurant, make your reservation by telephone at least two weeks in advance. Some restaurants need to be booked months in advance. If you are not familiar with the food or the layout, check out both before the big day. You don't want to find yourself stuck behind a pillar or next to a noisy serving station. Ask the captain for the numbers of the best tables in the house. This way, when you call, if the one you want isn't available, you can request a second choice.

What to Wear

A man who knows how to dress is sexy. If you think that putting on your best pair of jeans and cleanest plaid shirt is knowing how to dress, think again. Keep in mind the atmosphere of the restaurant. If you will be taking her to an upscale establishment with white tablecloths and a host or hostess to greet you, wear a jacket and a tie. They're too constricting? For which women's garment of torture would you trade—brassiere? Pantyhose? Pointy-toed, four-inch stiletto shoes created by masochistic designers? Be her equal and learn to endure.

Odd Stuff

- Even if you will be going to a moderately priced restaurant, take care how you dress. Dressing carelessly diminishes the occasion and devalues her.

- Hats are removed when entering someone's home and when sitting down to eat.

- Give away your baseball and trucker caps to a children's home. Never wear them at a dinner table, no matter how casual the restaurant.

- Keep elbows off the table when there is food in front of you. It's okay between courses and during dessert when the atmosphere is more relaxed.

In the Restaurant

If there is a host or hostess, he or she will lead you to your table; the woman follows, then you. If a host isn't present, you lead the way. Seat the lady in the best seat. It is usually the one facing into the restaurant. However, if there is a lovely view, seat your companion facing out. Usually the wait staff will pull out a chair for the woman. If not, learn to feel comfortable performing this courtesy. Pull the chair out. The woman will bend her knees to sit down. Hold the back of the chair with both hands and put your foot underneath to ensure that the chair doesn't tilt back. Make sure not to pull the chair back before sliding it under her in order to avoid her falling to the floor. Then push the chair forward using your hands and a knee together. Much of the time, all you need to do is stand behind her chair, and touch the back of it. Since you can't actually move it once she's sitting, your lady will be doing most of the work.

Enter your chair from its right side, and your left side, unless there is an obstacle in the way. This avoids people from colliding with one another. The woman is seated to your right.

Ordering the Food

Menus at tony restaurants have two sections: One is the *table d'hôte* (*tabl dote*), which has a preset succession of courses at a set price, and could be from a three- to a thirteen-course meal selection.

A three-course meal:

1. Appetizer or soup
2. Main meal
3. Dessert

A four-course meal:
1. Appetizer or soup
2. Fish
3. Main meal
4. Dessert

A seven-course meal:
1. Cold appetizer
2. Soup
3. Fish
4. Main meal
5. Salad
6. Sweets and cheese
7. Fruit

The à la carte menu offers the diner a choice of foods at individual, and usually higher, prices.

Ordering food with aplomb makes you look in control. Make suggestions regarding appetizers, soups, salads, and desserts in order to guide the woman as to the extent of your hospitality and of your budget. A smart woman will hear you suggesting the filet mignon, not the chicken special, and will choose accordingly. A dynamic entertainer asks the woman what she'd like to eat, and then gives both their orders to the server.

Ordering the Wine

Ask if she prefers red, white, or rosé, but you do the ordering. Most upscale restaurants have a sommelier (so mal yā′). Don't hesitate to ask for his or her informed suggestions. If your date doesn't care to drink wine, offer other choices for the beverage. When water is the choice, pass up tap water and order a bottle of sparkling or still (non-effervescent). When the wine steward brings the bottle of wine for you to taste, he or she will present the bottle with the label up to ensure that you received what you ordered, then will pour a small amount into your glass for you to taste. Check to see that the wine is at the right temperature and not spoiled; the woman's glass will be filled, then yours. Once you have approved the bottle, it is not proper to send it back.

Restaurant Staff

Well-trained staff will be quick to notice that you need their assistance. If you find yourself in a restaurant that is understaffed or poorly run, and you need to get someone's attention, snapping your fingers or waving your arms is not the way to do it. A small hand gesture, waiting to catch the server's eye, or calling "Waiter" or "Waitress" is appropriate. People serving you are not referred to as "Sir" or "Miss."

If there is a complaint with the food preparation, make the correction, but do it politely. If there is a problem with the service, notify the manager. You are paying for good food and for good service. Your tip is recognition and a reward for both. Not leaving a tip may result in the server running after you on your way out the door. Instead, leave just a token amount 5 percent to 10 percent, and the message will be received.

Odd Stuff

- Women know that only losers stiff a server of his or her proper tip.

Conversation

On a first-time date, it's the kiss of death to talk about your divorce, ex-wife, or past romances. Put off discussing your agoraphobia, your politics, or your ulcer. The best way to start a conversation is to ask a question: "How long have you been a real estate investor?" Or make a statement: "I had a great day at the office," or a combination compliment and a question: "You know a lot about the city. How long have you lived here?" Small talk is the best way to discover mutual interests that may lead to more intimate possibilities. Be well-informed on current events, television shows, books, the theater, sports. Talk about family and friends, your job, hobbies, places you have traveled, and your personal interests. Do unusual things like bungee jumping and parachuting, and then talk about your experiences.

It is flattering to a woman when you focus on her interests as well as on your own. Does she ski? What a coincidence—so do you. Without seeming to pry, and with sincere interest, ask the reporter's mainstay questions of who, what, when, where, why and how. Don't monopolize the conversation by talking only about yourself. Give her the opportunity to join in. Brush your hand on hers once or twice during the evening. Smile. Lean toward her. Make good eye contact at least 60 percent of the time, then look away, so as not to appear to stare. Nod your head. To be a good conversationalist, you need to be a good listener. Concentrate on her, not on your food. What you do nonverbally matters as much as what you say.

OUT ON THE TOWN

When I was fifteen years old and decided to embark on a quest of self-improvement, I asked myself what it is that cultured people do. I decided that they listened to classical music, spoke French, and played tennis. I bought my first Tchaikovsky album *The 1812 Overture* from a subway vendor, and became hooked on great music for life. The French and tennis followed later.

Concerts, Theater, Opera and Ballet

If the only culture in your house is growing on the bathroom floors and kitchen counters, it's time to reconsider your lifestyle. To be truly cultured, find out why the names of the three Bs, (Brahms, Beethoven, and Bach) have lasted down through the centuries, but the names of most popular performers rarely last past their generation.

Tickets for the theater, the opera, and the ballet can be pricey, but they usually sell out quickly, so it's a good idea to book two or three months in advance. Keep your budget in mind, but remember that economizing on the price of the ticket can place you behind a huge pole or in the nosebleed section. Metropolitan cities have telephone directories with seating charts for theaters and stadiums. Check the Internet or ask when you place your order where the best seats are for what you can spend.

Basic good theater manners require that you don't behave the way some do at a football game. Get to your seats early, before the curtain rises, don't talk after the performance has begun, not even in a whisper, or eat or drink at your seats. Being annoying to the people around you and to the performers is rude.

What people wear usually reflects the price of the seats, but no matter what your budget is, it is tasteless to arrive at a theater carelessly dressed in jeans and sweat shirt. A dress suit, white shirt and a tie work well in higher-priced sections.

At cultural performances, arriving late is boorish. Even worse, you will be required to watch the first act in the lobby on a television screen. When a man and a woman attend the theater together, the man goes first with the tickets, but when they reach their places he steps aside and lets the woman enter the row first. A woman never takes the aisle seat when she is with a man.

Who goes down the aisle first is a matter of convenience. When several people attend the theater together, they should determine before going down the aisle how they are to sit and go down the aisle in that order, so that there will be less disturbance to others when they reach their places. When leaving the theater, women precede men back up the aisle.

Talking during the performance, shifting your body, moving your head from side to side and rustling your program is disturbing to others. Learn when to applaud. Usually, you should clap only at the end of a scene, an act, or when the music is finished. Devotees know when that is. Applauding before the end will give you away as a novice. If you're not familiar with the performance, don't applaud until everyone else does.

Standing ovations are fine at a rock concert, but it is rude to stand up to applaud so that others cannot see. Should you decide to shout "Bravo!" make sure the object of your admiration is a male performer. Say "Brava!" for a woman.

It shows bad breeding and thoughtlessness for the artists for people to leave immediately after the curtain has fallen, and even worse, before the performance is over, without showing their appreciation. Your car will probably still be where you parked it. Wait and applaud those who have given so much of themselves to entertain you for the evening.

Odd Stuff

- In boxes at the theater or the opera, if you are with another couple, the two ladies sit up front and each man sits directly behind his partner.

- Set the standards for others by extending courtesies to a woman. Help her into her coat by holding it halfway on the collar. Position the sleeves so that it is easy for her to locate and slip her hand into one, and then the other, and lift the coat onto her shoulders. Lift it again to position it comfortably on her clothing.

ENDING THE DATE

If you have made arrangements to meet at the restaurant instead of picking her up at her home, offer to take your date home, either in a cab or in your car. If she decides to take a cab, you are not obligated to pay the fare. If you drive her home and you are asked in, don't assume it will be for anything else except coffee. If you are not asked in, kiss her on the cheek in your car, thank her for an enjoyable evening, walk her to her door, say good night, and wait until she is safely inside before leaving.

Your date will make it very clear if she wants to see you again.

CHAPTER 2
HOSTING A SOCIAL DINNER AT HOME

Image is crucial to success.

—Benjamin Franklin

When a new president and first lady entertain at the White House, their first international guests are not the heads of state of large nations, but of smaller ones. This gives them the opportunity to learn the ropes, practice, and work out the bugs. You have to do the same.

The secret of hosting a great dinner party lies in making your guests feel comfortable. If you are relaxed and have everything under control, others will sense it. As in everything in life—sports, music, or building a house—entertaining takes practice, so you might begin by inviting your family and closest friends to a get-together, and practice on them. Begin with a meal that you have prepared several times for your self. Make it your "specialty." Above all, get your timing down. Start out with a three-course dinner—soup or salad, main meal, and coffee and dessert. If you must, order a quart of delicious soup from a restaurant, and simply heat it up the night of your soirée.

Attend a cooking class. Many upscale food markets offer them weekly on-site. You will not only impress your guests with your new talents, but it's also a wonderful venue for meeting women. You can also attend wine-tasting classes there. Ask friends and relatives for their favorite recipes of five or fewer ingredients, or cut them out from the newspaper.

Cook a casserole that can be prepared a day ahead, and heat it in the microwave oven. Keep things simple, but when possible have a choice available. Offer regular or decaffeinated coffee, or tea; cream, lemon, sugar or artificial sweetener; a sinful dessert or exotic fruit. Sit back and bask in the compliments. Once you feel comfortable with your success, you're ready to move on to more challenging fare.

THE INVITATION

Telephone or mail invitations two to four weeks in advance. The less formal the event, the less lead time you need. The kind of invitation you send depends on the kind of party you're having. A telephone invitation is fine for informal dinners with close friends. Sending more formal, fold-over invitations shows a little more class.

Give the time, date and location, of your party, and what to wear. Too many misguided people think that casual means T-shirts, shorts, and sandals. Don't be cryptic. People shouldn't have to interpret what you expect in terms of dress. It's always a good idea to have a theme, but be creative. Toga parties are okay for a college crowd, but sophisticates expect to attend something much more creative.

You decide if you want invitees to bring food or drink, and if you wish to accommodate the friend of a friend. Consider the space you have available and your budget. When you are having a couples party, it is appropriate to invite the partner with whom a friend is living, since they are considered a twosome. You make that understood when you state "and guest." If you're not inviting the children of friends, make it clear at the time you call or write. Say that you're having a get-together, and hope that your friends can find a sitter for the evening, *so that they can attend*. Do the same for their pets.

When people haven't responded to your invitation within a week to ten days, call them and say that you're checking to make sure that they received your invitation.

✦ ✦ ✦

It belongs to the chiefest in the company to unfold his napkin and fall to meat first.

—George Washington

✦ ✦ ✦

SETTING THE TABLE

Taking the time to set an appealing and proper table is the hallmark of men of class, and a compliment to your guests. Your place setting doesn't have to be lavish, just handsomely presented. The rules of setting the table are simple. A complete dish set, cloth napkins, odd pieces of silverware, and crystal can be bought at a flea market or resale shop for a fraction of their original costs. It's a gracious gesture and less disruptive to have the table ready before your guests arrive. Use a tablecloth—it adds a touch of class. Just remember to iron out the folds. It is better to let the table go bare than to use placemats, which are generally more appropriate for informal lunches. Candlelight and a centerpiece add to the attractiveness of the setting, but make sure that they aren't too tall so that people don't have to talk around and over them.

Place Cards

Place cards are useful when there are many guests. Even at an informal party of six or more, it's a good idea to use place cards at a dinner where people don't know each other. This gives them an opportunity to glance at them and remember the names of the people they are talking to. Place cards should be handwritten in pen and centered at the top of the cover plate. For an informal dinner, first names only are sufficient. For a formal dinner, use the person's title (Mr., Ms., Dr., etc.) and last name.

THE MESS

No, not your living quarters! In fourteenth-century England, food was not passed at the table. Instead, two couples chose what to eat from a commonly shared "mess," or portion of food that was placed between them on platters. A "cover" referred to a lord's food, which was covered with cloth to keep the food warm or to prevent possible poisoning while being carried from the distant kitchen to the table.

French aristocrats placed a slice of hard bread—a *tranche*—on the table before each guest as a means of sopping up drippings from their dinner, since plates were not yet in vogue. This bread trencher was later distributed as food to the poor who camped outside the lord's manor. The bread trencher eventually morphed into one of wood, then metal, then ceramic, and came down to us as a very large plate known as the "place plate," "charger," or "cover plate."

Dishes and Napkins

Cover Plate

Putting the large cover plate on the table before your guests arrive serves as a place marker, as well as avoids people from having to sit down at an empty place setting. Today we allow sixteen to twenty inches of room for each guest's space. This space is now called the "cover," from which we derive the term "cover charge" when we go to a restaurant. Remove the cover plate along with the first-course dish when that course is finished.

Soup Plate

There is a difference between a soup plate and a soup bowl. The *soup plate* is shallow and has a rim. When you are finished eating from a soup plate, you may leave the spoon inside the well if the underplate is small. A *soup bowl* is used for informal dining. When you have finished eating from a soup bowl, put the spoon on the under plate.

Dinner Plate

Your dinner plate acts as the central point of decorating the table. If you have a simple dish pattern, contrast the plain design with just two ornate accents in the linens and in the tableware. To change the look of the table, mix and match the soup, salad and dessert plates based on the dinner plate. For flow, the cups and saucers should be of the same design as the dinner plate. For an ornate dinner plate, contrast the design with two simple accents in the linens and the tableware.

Place dinner plates one inch from the edge of the table, with the motif, if there is one, facing toward your guests. Never use chipped or cracked dishes.

Salad Plate

If you are serving salad as a first course, set the salad plate on the cover plate, if you are using one. When serving salad with the main meal, set it to the left of the dinner plate, above the forks.

Bread and Butter Plate

The bread and butter plate is placed to the left of the dinner plate, above or to the side of the forks. The butter spreader is placed either horizontally across the upper edge, or vertically on the right of the plate, with the blade facing in.

Set out a quarter-stick of butter at each end of the table; for a long table, set one in the center, too. Once the food is on the plates, guests should be able to help themselves without interrupting the flow of their conversation by asking that something be passed. At a formal dinner, bread is placed directly on the table.

Cup and Saucer

A cup and saucer are placed on the table, along with the dessert plate, after the dinner dishes have been cleared.

Napkins

It is the responsibility of the host to put his napkin on his lap to indicate that the meal is about to begin. The dinner napkin is approximately twenty-two inches to thirty inches square. Use cloth. Place the napkin folded into a rectangle farthest on the table to the left of the dinner plate, with the fold facing the plate. Don't place any silverware on the napkin. That would necessitate moving the silverware off the napkin in order to place the napkin on your lap. Otherwise, place the napkin directly on the dinner plate, with the fold on the right. Napkins are not placed on the table for show. They are to be picked up and used! If you have to leave the table during the meal, place your napkin on your seat, not back on the table so that others won't have to look at it, and as a signal to the server that you will be returning.

Silverware

Silverware is placed in the order that it will be used. The amount of silverware you place on a table depends on the number of courses you will be serving. It isn't nice to trick your guests, so don't place any more pieces on the table than what you'll actually be using. There is no need to place a salad fork on the table if you serve salad along with the main meal, not as a separate course.

Align silverware pieces about one inch from the edge of the table.

Knives

In the Middle Ages, when hosts were not expected to provide cutlery for their guests, men of the nobility took special food knives with them when they went to dine. They had the dual purpose of a dagger, and of cutting pieces of meat for couples to share. In the sixteenth century, the Italians began to use knives for the sole purpose of eating.

Renaissance men sometimes took the occasion of a dinner filled with liquor, debate, and bawdy behavior to impolitely stab a fellow guest. In seventeenth-century France, knives with pointed tips were outlawed in an attempt to staunch the rise in dinnertime violence. In their place came single-edged knives with the cutting edge facing in. The thinking was, if the blade faced in, there was less likelihood of getting a good shot at a tablemate. These traditions carry on to this very day, where only the steak knife has a point. It's also the reason a woman is seated between two men.

No more than three knives should be placed to the right of the plate at any one time—for example, the fish, meat, and salad knives. The butter knife is placed on the butter service plate. It is used to take the butter from the butter dish to place it on individual butter plates. The butter spreader spreads the butter on the bread. Place other knives at the setting as needed as you are serving that course. Don't place a knife if you can do without one.

Forks

Sophisticates from seventeenth century Italy spread the use of individual forks throughout Europe. After some unsuccessful attempts in England, the fork ultimately gained European acceptance when it was made fashionable in France, by Catherine de'Medici. Its shape morphed between two and four prongs; the rich used a different fork to eat and serve every food, but mostly confusion existed with how to properly manipulate it. When the new craze finally reached America, it did not come with instructions, and Americans simply created their own.

Forks are placed to the left of the dinner plate. (The exception is the cocktail/oyster fork, which is placed to the right of the soup spoon.) The fork to be used first is placed farthest from the plate. The other forks follow in the order of their use. The salad fork is a rover. If it's placed to the left of the main meal fork, then the salad course is to being served before the main course, American style. If it's placed to the right of the main meal fork, the salad course is being served after the main meal, European style.

If more pieces are needed, they are brought in when the food is served. For example, a dessert fork, if needed, is brought in with dessert when it is served. Otherwise it is preplaced horizontally above the main dish plate, European style, in order to skirt around the numbers rule.

Spoons

Spoons got their original inspiration from the cupped hand. Like knives, spoons are placed on the right of the plate. Since the soup spoon is used before any knife, it is placed farthest from the plate, and may be the only spoon on the table for the initial place setting. Coffee spoons are brought in with the coffee. Hold the spoon like a pencil to eat soup and to stir tea, coffee, or cocoa. After stirring your beverage, and testing it for sweetness and temperature, lay the spoon on the saucer behind the handle of the cup. Do not leave it sticking up in the cup.

For iced tea, after stirring, place the iced-tea spoon on the underplate or coaster if there is one. If there isn't one, hold the spoon with the first two fingers of your hand against the inside rim of the glass while drinking. Leave the spoon in the glass when you have finished.

The dessert spoon can be brought in when dessert is served, together with the finger bowl, or it can be preplaced horizontally, European style, above the plate along with the dessert fork. Place the spoon above the fork with its handle facing to the right. The fork's handle faces to the left.

♦ ♦ ♦

Beyond all doubt there is a certain pre-established harmony between different wines and different shapes and sizes of glasses.

—George Saintsbury

♦ ♦ ♦

Glasses

With the establishment of Venetian glass-blowing skills in the sixteenth century, glass replaced pottery and metal cups and goblets in refined dining. Glasses are placed to the right of the dinner plate, above the knives and spoons. The water glass is placed above the tip of the dinner knife. A white-wine glass is smaller than a red-wine glass, and is placed in front of the red-wine glass, because it is used first. White- and red-wine glasses also have different shapes. If budget is a consideration, purchase medium, all-purpose wineglasses. They don't all have to match, but use your creativity in order for them to coordinate with one another. When you can, move up to crystal. Crystal lends a touch of elegance to the evening. Its intrinsic beauty enhances appreciation of the wine it holds. If you have perfect pitch, a good ring is in F or G sharp.

Table space may be a consideration. For a formal dinner, place no more than four glasses—water, white-wine, red-wine, and champagne glasses, above the place setting. If you decide to serve sherry, the sherry glass is placed on the outside right of the others. If not, place the white-wine glass there. When you are using a champagne glass, to conserve space, place it behind the grouping.

For an informal dinner, it is customary to place no more than three glasses. Offer a clean glass each time you change the wine. If you will be serving brandy with coffee, set the glasses out at the time you serve it.

Appetizer and dessert wines are served in a stemmed glass, ranging from three to five ounces.

Light dinner wines are served in a medium glass, ranging from five to twelve ounces. Hold a white-wine glass by the stem only. The bowl is warmed when the glass is cupped, which defeats the purpose of keeping the white wine at a cool temperature.

Bordeaux   Burgundy   White wine   Champagne   Brandy   Sherry

Red dinner wines are served in a larger glass, ranging from eight to twelve ounces. A red-wine glass may be held where the stem and the bowl meet, but the fingers must still be kept on the stem. Red wine is heartier than white, and better if it chambered. The glass should allow you two ways to enjoy the experience. It should be clear and free of decorations, so you are able to see the color and clarity of the wine; it should be large enough for you to swirl the wine and smell the bouquet.

Brandy is served in a 4½-inch-high snifter, holding one to two ounces. A brandy glass has almost no stem and is cupped, so that you can warm it by the heat of the hand, which helps release the bouquet.

PLAN AHEAD

The course of food you choose should have a balance between light and heavy texture, sweet and sour taste, hot and cold temperature, crisp and smooth, and a contrast of color. When choosing which of the courses you want to serve, remember to alter the consistencies of the food. For example, after a light soup or seafood cocktail, follow it by a heavier hot meat course; next, serve a crisp salad with a vinaigrette dressing, followed by a sweet dessert.

If you are going to serve drinks before dinner, prepare to have enough for at least two drinks for each person.

Include wine, aperitifs, soft drinks, juice, and water in your selection. Serve drinks before dinner, away from the eating table, one hour before dinner starts. Have readily available glasses and a bucket or bowl filled with ice. Make up a dessert tray ahead of time, with coffee cups, spoons, forks, sugar bowl and a small pitcher of cream or milk. Have the coffee maker ready to be switched on. If you're going to have music and dancing, set up to have soft themes during dinner, then gradually move on to more and more lively selections as the evening progresses.

SEATING GUESTS

Seating guests properly is an art. Guests should not be told to "just sit anywhere." You, as the host, decide who will be compatible table partners. You might sit a quiet person who prefers to listen next to an extrovert who loves to talk. Males and females should be seated alternately, in order to avoid gender-oriented subjects from entering into the conversation. Women are seated to the right of men, because a woman "on the left" is not esteemed. Husbands and wives are not seated next to one another. You choose who the "most important" male guest is, then seat that person's female companion next to you, on your right-hand side. The second most important female guest is seated on your left.

When having several guests for dinner, an unpaired male host might ask a female friend to act as hostess. The hostess sits at the other end with the most important male guest on her right and the second most important male guest on her left.

If you have dinner guests in numbers divisible by 2, e.g., 4, 6, 10, alternate them by male-female.

	Female Guest 2	Male Guest 1	
Host			Female Co-host
	Female Guest 1	Male Guest 2	

This arrangement does not work with numbers divisible by 4, e.g., 8, 12, 16. In order to retain the alternate male-female seating; you and your female co-host do not sit opposite each other.

She sits "down" one chair to the left of the table, and the male guest 1 now sits facing the host.

	Female Guest 2	Male Guest 3	Female Guest 3	
Host				Male Guest 1
	Female Guest 1	Male Guest 2	Female Co-host	

For a gathering of six or fewer, when it is time to be seated, direct your guests to their seats yourself. For a larger group, put out place cards. Except for engaged couples, arrange it so that couples don't sit side by side with each other. The point of the dinner should be camaraderie and the exchange of lively conversation. It is presumed that couples who know each other are also familiar with each other's stories.

Try not to have an uneven number of people at the table in order that each will have someone to talk to. Five people are the most awkward of all. In some countries, it is thought to be bad luck to have thirteen at the table. If someone cancels at the last minute, be ready to have a neighbor, a co-worker, or a relative pinch-hit. If there is an extra person, sit two of the same sex next to each other as in the illustration below, where there is an extra man.

	Female Guest 2	Male Guest 3	Male Guest 1	
Host				Hostess
	Female Guest 1		Male Guest 2	

STARTING THE MEAL

There are still people who know not to begin eating until the person acting as hostess picks up her fork as a signal for everyone to start eating, or suggests that guests begin the meal "before everything gets cold."

Throughout the meal, take responsibility for directing the conversation and leading the group in current, hot, or amusing topics. Introduce subjects that you know each guest has some expertise in, or are of special interest. This gives each guest an opportunity to shine, but don't let any one guest dominate the conversation for too long. Switch the subject if someone is becoming argumentative. Make sure guests don't become involved in heated discussions or in word games.

SERVING THE DINNER

Sit at the end of the table closest to the kitchen for all the getting up you will be doing. An informal way to start the meal is to have the food on a buffet-type table and have your guests serve themselves before sitting down. Or, if you don't already have the first course in place, bring the food to the table, preplated. This avoids the appearance of a family-style meal. Socially, women are served before men. During medieval times, the proper host served the hostess first, in order to prove to his guests that the food wasn't poisoned.

We've come a long way from then, but it's always courteous and never incorrect to serve the lady on your right first.

Fill the wineglasses of the ladies at your end. After the first glasses of wine are finished, encourage one of the gentlemen at the other end of the table to do the honors there, while you refill the glasses of those seated nearest you. If you have served soup, salad follows the main course.

Soup

The first course—if it is soup—is put on the cover plate. The soup plate or bowl should be filled to less than half, since you don't want to appear to be filling up your guests on it. Wine is usually not served with soup, but if you wish, serve a sherry. When soup is finished, remove the cover plate and the soup plate together, and place the next course.

The reason we "eat" our soup is at early English banquets, meat stews with their liquids were served in bowls. Couples brought their own knives and spoons and shared one bowl.

Salad

If you are serving salad as the first course, remove the cover plate and place the salad dish and the dinner plate. When everyone has finished, remove the salad dish, along with the fork. If you plan to serve a plated dinner from the kitchen, take the dinner plate with you, too. Otherwise, leave the dinner plate, and serve the next course and its side dishes at the table, where guests serve themselves.

Fish

If you wish to be elaborate, the third course may be fish. To keep to a three-course meal, omit the fish and follow with the main meat course and side dishes. You will, of course, have previously checked on who is or isn't a vegetarian and if guests have any allergies.

Main Meal

The main meal is what the other courses center around. Balance courses to incorporate and contrast the four Ts—(color) tone, texture, temperature, and taste.

Tone

We eat with our eyes. Introduce complementary colors to add to the appeal of what you are serving. A meal of broccoli with hollandaise sauce, buttered carrots, and chicken with cranberry sauce is more visually appealing than a monochromatic dish of white cauliflower, white mashed potatoes and chicken covered in white cream gravy.

Texture

> Serve a crisp food with one that is soft, a bland flavor with spicy food. If you have served a hearty main meal, serve a light dessert. A light meal calls for a rich dessert.

Taste

> Usually, one highly seasoned food per meal is enough. Serve only one starchy food at each meal such as potatoes, rice, pasta, or corn.

Temperature

> Contrast hot foods with a cold food served with the main course. Serve hot foods hot and cold foods cold. Warmed and chilled plates add a special touch.

Cheese

On a large platter, arrange a variety of three to five cheeses in a range of flavors from mild to strong, textures from soft to hard, and styles domestic and foreign. Supply a separate knife for soft and hard cheeses, and garnish the platter with fruits such as papaya as pears, kiwi, or grapes. Serve with wine and hard bread or crackers.

- Serve at room temperature between 68 and 72 degrees Fahrenheit.
- Cheese balls are cut in half, then into wedges.
- Round or half-round cheeses are cut in wedges.
- Wedge-shaped cheeses are cut crosswise from the tip to about two-thirds in; the rest is cut lengthwise. With a wedge, slice it lengthwise, not a slice across the tip.

Dessert

Before serving dessert, clear off the table. Our word *dessert* comes from the French verb *desservir*—to clear off. Take away the dinner plates, the forks and knives, serving bowls, and the salt and pepper shakers. Don't let volunteers help to stack dishes or clear the table. If people get up to help, the mood of the party may be lost. Don't start loading the dishwasher until everyone has gone home.

When the table is cleared, bring a third bottle of wine and the dessert tray to the table. If you are serving coffee, bring that out, too.

For dessert with a sauce, you will need to provide both a spoon and a fork. Bring in your dessert accompanied by the spoon and the fork, or you may preplace the dessert fork and spoon above the plate.

After dessert and coffee, let people help themselves to wine, but *it is your responsibility not to let anyone go home drunk.* Allow the party to wind down naturally.

Coffee

In the United States, people drink coffee either with their meals or with their dessert. In Europe, if Champagne is served with dessert, coffee is served as a separate course. When entertaining, it is more correct to offer coffee after the plates of dessert have been served. In formal entertaining, demitasse coffee is served as a separate course, often in another room of the house, in demitasse cups and with small spoons, when sugar is requested.

Have on hand:

- Coffee or decaffeinated coffee
- Milk or half-and-half
- Sugar or artificial sweetener (serve the sugar in a bowl with a small spoon, or sugar lumps in a bowl with small tongs; the sweetener is served in its packets in an attractive bowl). Both sugar and artificial sweetener should be served on the same tray.

Coffee may be served at the dining table or in a separate room. Changing rooms allows guests to circulate and to talk to people they were not sitting next to at dinner;

however, it may also have the unwanted effect of breaking the convivial mood of the moment. The quaint custom of the men remaining behind in the dining room when coffee was served to puff their Havanas and talk politics while the women retreated from the smoke to the "withdrawing room" with their coffee is déclassé.

Odd Stuff

- When serving tea or coffee, the liquid is poured first. Then milk, cream, lemon or sugar is added.
- Hold the cup between your fingers and thumb; do not curl the fingers around the handle.
- Do not slurp or taste the brew from the spoon.
- Remove the spoon from the cup and place it alongside it on the saucer.
- Don't lick the spoon.
- The emptied packets of sweetener or sugar are folded in half and tucked under the edge of the saucer.
- Serve food and drink in a counterclockwise direction. Begin with the person at your right and end with yourself. It's a good idea to have serving dishes at each end of the table.

- Traditionally, an after-dinner liqueur is served away from the table. At an informal dinner, it is acceptable to just remove the plates, and serve liqueur at the table.

- If you are aspiring to be in "society," it's a good idea to have hired help to coordinate and serve the dinner if there are more than eight people. If you're on a budget, a neighborhood teenager may be commandeered into helping serve the appetizers, the main meal, dessert, etc. A local culinary school also can be a gold mine for finding qualified assistance.

❖ ❖ ❖

To be successful, do something better than anyone else.

—Unknown

❖ ❖ ❖

MAKING THE TOAST

In medieval Europe, it was rare for each person to have his or her own glass at the table. The tradition of toasting comes from the old British practice of floating a piece of toasted bread on top of the wine or ale in the communal loving cup. Once the loving cup had been passed around, the host drank the remainder of the wine and ate the toast that had sunk to the bottom of the glass, in honor of his guests. An early English form of a toast was "Let us hob and nob," roughly meaning "Let us give and take." When you're hobnobbing, it now means that you're clinking glasses with people of the upper classes.

The accomplished host uses the opening of the main meal to welcome all his guests with a toast. If you feel comfortable about it, stand up, raise your glass, and give the toast in a general welcome. It is not necessary to make a long-winded speech (thirty seconds will do), or to clink glasses afterward. If there is a guest of honor, a second toast is given after dessert is served. If you don't feel comfortable giving a toast, ask someone else (ahead of time) to do the honors.

DEPARTURE

It's a compliment to you if your guests never want to go home, but you can prepare them for leaving by explaining that you have an early appointment in the morning and you'll have to "close shop" in fifteen or twenty minutes. Your announcement gives everyone the chance to finish a drink or a conversation, and mentally gear up for departure. If people still don't get the hint, start clearing away the liquor.

Odd Stuff

- Match the colors of a flowered centerpiece to the colors of the table linen and the china.

- When wineglasses are being filled, they are left on the table, not lifted up.

- Don't accept any telephone calls during dinner.

- The under plate is the dish placed under a cup or bowl.

- If something breaks, don't accept an offer to replace the item. Breakage and spills come with the territory.

- When a guest brings something that you don't wish to serve with your dinner, thank him or her, and state that you will enjoy it at another time. If the gift blends with your menu, you may choose to serve it as part of your dinner.

- Some hosts welcome help in the kitchen, others don't want any. At an informal party, it's up to you.

- If you say grace before meals, and you wish to give this honor to a guest, don't spring it on the person after he or she sits down at the table. Ask ahead of time to avoid embarrassment, if the person might be uncomfortable. When a religious leader is one of your dinner guests, he or she should always be asked to do the honor. If you are unsure of the religion of your guests, or if they are of diverse faiths, offer a generic prayer.

- The appropriate amount of time to wait dinner for a late guest is fifteen minutes. Longer than twenty minutes is inconsiderate to those who came on time.

BUFFETS

If there is space, place the buffet table away from the wall in order to avoid a bottleneck. When setting a buffet, lay out the dinner plate and the main meal dish at one end of the table. Place other foods and serving pieces within easy reach at the middle of the table, with the bread, butter, relishes, and salt and pepper at the far end. Leave room for your friends to put down their plates next to each serving dish. Place silverware and napkins at the other end of the table where they are picked up last. If space is limited, set up a cart for beverages, cups and glasses, cream and sugar. No need to make an announcement when you are ready to serve. Go up and invite people a few at a time.

For a seated fork buffet, a cold starter can be plated in advance and placed at each setting before everyone sits down. Guests can then help themselves to the main course and dessert. If you have space, set up a separate area for dessert to assist with clearing away. Don't put the beverage area next to the buffet. This can cause congestion.

If your budget allows, engage a caterer to prepare and serve the food.

COCKTAIL PARTIES

Cocktail parties are an excellent way to entertain lots of people and meet all your outstanding social obligations at the same time. Invite guests for anytime starting from 5:30 to 7:30 P.M. to allow time to arrive after work.

The number of people you invite depends on your budget and how many can comfortably fit into your living space. Don't crowd people. Push furniture against the walls, and set up tables to hold the food, the bar, and a place to put empty glasses. Have small baskets to hold used napkins, uneaten foodstuff and toothpicks.

For a two-hour event, serve bite-size snacks and canapés that do not need a plate. Allow three or four canapés per person if guests are going off to dinner; allow six to eight per person if you've invited them for two hours. Pace the food. Ask friends or professional waiting staff to help pass the trays, and have plenty of cocktail napkins and toothpicks available. Start with cold canapés and move to hot. End the party with sweet canapés such as strawberries dipped in chocolate.

THE BAR

If you will be mixing drinks yourself, keep everything simple. Have on hand: vodka, whiskey, tequila, rum, gin or scotch; red and white wine; beer; nonalcoholic drinks of colas, orange and tomato juice and bottled water; and garnishes of lemon wedges, olives, maraschino cherries, cocktail onions, and celery stalks.

A half-hour after the stated end time on the invitation, close down the bar and ask musicians to leave or turn off the music.

CHAPTER 3
HOW TO DINE

There are two things to aim at in life: first to get what you want; and after that, to enjoy it.

—Logan Pearsall Smith

Your table manners might arguably be the single most important indicator of your breeding. The most telling aspect of your table etiquette is how well you have conquered the manipulation of the various eating utensils and how you finesse difficult-to-eat foods. If you were not fortunate to attend a Swiss finishing school, you've already made a good start by reading this book. Other ways to learn proper table manners is by observing people who use them themselves, by watching old movies, and asking friends to critique you when you are eating together. It isn't necessary to know and practice esoteric details of eating, but fisting your cutlery like a caveman, leaving bits of masticated food on your drinking glass, or displaying a mouth full of food while talking just won't do.

THE PLACE SETTING

The place setting tells people at a glance how many courses are being served, so that they can pace how much food to eat at each course. Learn where things go in the place setting so that you won't be eating your neighbor's salad or drinking someone else's coffee. Solids, such as bread and salads, are placed on the upper left of the dinner plate. You have to reach across your plate to get at them. Liquids such as water, wine, and coffee are placed to the upper right of the plate.

THE COURSES OF FOOD

A typical three-course meal could be soup, fish, and dessert; appetizer, meat, and salad; or salad, meat, and dessert. The following course structure is for seven-course dining, when the place setting is preset on the table. Naturally, you chose how many courses you wish to have for your meal.

First Course
Seafood Cocktail

> The first course may be a seafood cocktail. The seafood cocktail fork is the only fork placed on the right side of the plate, either with the fork tines in the soupspoon bowl and the handle at a 45-degree angle, or is laid parallel to the soupspoon.

Second Course
Soup

> Soup should be served at a formal dinner. The soupspoon is placed to the right side of the outside knife. If you order soup as a separate course, the spoon will be brought in with the soup. In a private home, do not ask for second helpings of the soup course, there may not be any.

Third Course
Fish

For a fish course, a notched fork is placed on the left side of your plate and a knife on the right. The fish knife has a notch cut out of it on its right side and a somewhat pointed tip. The purpose of this tip is to help remove bones. Fish bones are removed with the thumb and index finger, and then put on the edge of the plate. In a private home, don't ask for a second helping.

Fourth Course
The Entrée (Main Meal)

In Europe, the entrée is what we call the appetizer; in the United States the entrée is often considered the main meal, so you will find at your place setting a dinner fork on the left of your plate and a dinner knife on the right side.

Fifth Course
Salad

If salad is served as a separate course after the entrée, there will be a smaller fork on the left, and a smaller knife on the right, next to your plate. The server will place the salad plate in front of you. At an informal dinner, the salad plate is already on the table—to the left of your forks—when you approach the table at the beginning of the meal. Eat the salad with the same fork that you are using to eat the main meal.

Sixth Course
Coffee and Dessert

A dessert spoon and a fork may be placed above the dinner plate. When dessert is served, the server will lay down your preplated dessert. Move the fork to the left and the spoon to the right of your plate. Alternately, the dessert fork and spoon may be brought to the table when the dessert is served.

To eat dessert when the spoon is needed, eat from the spoon held in the right hand. The fork is held in the left hand and is used only to push food onto the spoon.

Traditionally, sparkling wine is served with dessert, with demitasse coffee served after dessert in another room, but usually both coffee and tea are served before, with, or during dessert.

Seventh Course
Fruit

In a multicourse dinner, fruit is served as the last course. If needed, a fruit knife and fork are brought in with the serving.

The Finger Bowl

After eating the fish or fruit courses, you may need to clean your hands. At an upscale dinner party or a good restaurant, you may be presented with a finger bowl before dessert. No need to panic. Follow these simple guidelines, and you'll be fine.

1. The server brings the finger bowl set on a doily, both of which sit on the dessert dish. They are placed in front of you with the fork and spoon set on the left and right of the dish, respectively.

2. Place the fork to the left of the dish and the spoon to the right of it.

3. Pick up the doily and the finger bowl, and set them above and to the left of the dessert dish, which is now ready to receive a serving of dessert.

4. When the dessert dish has been removed, pick up both the doily and the finger bowl and place them in front of you.

Dessert plate with finger bowl   *Dessert plate ready to receive dessert*

5. Dip just the tips of your fingers in the finger bowl. You may pat your lips with wet finger tips; bend and wipe your lips on the napkin held low on your lap.

6. Pat, don't rub, your fingers dry on your napkin.

If the finger bowl is brought in before a fruit course, you will be given a knife in place of the spoon.

Odd Stuff

- You might be served a tart fruit sorbet after fish to cleanse the palate. It is served in a small chilled cup. Eat the sorbet with the spoon that is brought in when it is served.

- In high-end restaurants, a lemon half for fish is covered with a cap of gauze to prevent the juice from spraying.

To protect yourself and others, cup your free hand over the lemon when squeezing it.

- Do not clink the sides of the cup when stirring tea or coffee.

STYLES OF EATING

During World War II, American spies often gave themselves away because of the way they held their cutlery. The knife and the fork are held the same way to cut food in both the American and the European styles of eating. What changes is how food is brought to the mouth with the fork, which remains the most incorrectly and creatively held utensil on the table. I prefer to eat in the European style, which is used in every country *except* the United States. It's quieter, easier, and more elegant.

European Style of Eating

1. Hold the fork in the open palm of your left hand, with the neck resting against the tip of your index finger. Hold the knife in the open palm of your right hand with the neck of the knife resting on your index finger. Support the handles with your thumb and middle fingers.

2. Curl your other fingers around the handles and turn your hands over. If you are left-handed, reverse the procedure.

3. Cut one piece of food at a time, and bring the fork, tines **down**, to your mouth. The knife, held one or two inches horizontal to the plate, stays in your right hand and may be used to push a small amount of vegetables onto the back of your fork.

4. When you wish to talk or reach for a beverage, place the knife blade across the plate with the handle pointing to four on the clock. Place the fork across the plate, tines **down** with the handle pointing to eight on the clock.

Resting *Finished*

5. When you have finished eating, place your knife and fork, tines **up or down**, with the handles pointing to four on the clock.

6. When eating with only the fork, it's acceptable to rest the free wrist or forearm against the edge of the table. At the end of the meal, place the fork on your plate with the tines **up** and the handle pointing to four on the clock.

American Zigzag Style of Eating

1. Food is cut the same way in the American style of eating as it is in the European style.

2. After cutting a piece of food, place your knife on the right rim of the plate and switch the fork to your right hand. Hold the fork like a pencil, tines **up,** with the handle between the middle and the index finger. Support the fork by placing the thumb on the handle and curling your fourth and fifth fingers in the palm of the hand, and eat.

3. To cut another piece of food, switch the fork back to your left hand; pick up the knife in the right hand, and reposition the knife and fork in the cutting position.

4. When you wish to talk or reach for a beverage, place your knife and fork separated from each other, fork tines **up**, with the handles pointing to the four on the clock. This is the resting position.

Resting *Finished*

5. When you have finished eating, place your knife and fork together, fork tines **up**, with the handles pointing to the four on the clock.

6. When eating with only the fork, the free hand is left resting on the lap. At the end of the meal, place it on the plate with the tines **up** and the handle in the four o'clock position.

Odd Stuff

- Don't fist the fork or hold it like a pitchfork or a cello. Don't use it to mash foods.

- When you're not using the knife and fork, rest them on the plate, not propped up on the table looking like oars in the water.

- The knife blade always faces the center of the plate.

EATING DAUNTING FOODS

It's difficult to concentrate on a social conversation or business negotiations when you're struggling with an unfamiliar meal. Avoid ordering foods that are difficult or messy to eat. Spaghetti and lobster are not good choices when meeting with clients. If you are served a prearranged meal, deal with daunting foods the best you can. Focus on the business at hand, not the food. Remember, at a business luncheon or dinner, you are not there to eat. Let the conversation take priority over the food. If you find yourself confronted with food that you cannot handle, leave it and concentrate on the reason you are there.

People who are prime candidates for top-level corporate positions are often taken out to lunch by the prospective employer who purposely orders difficult-to-eat food to gauge a candidate's ability to handle unexpected situations. A person under scrutiny might be given frog legs to eat. Are they eaten with the fingers, or are they cut with a knife and a fork?

At the negotiating level, corporations are not interested in embarking on a training program for beginners. They want men who can take off running, who are comfortable in high-powered social settings, and who can close the deal. If a candidate is not able to exude social competencies on a par with other world-class competitors and clients, they will simply find someone who can.

Employees for top positions may have to acquire membership into an exclusive club as a consideration for promotion. Candidates and their spouses are sometimes invited to dinner for the sole purpose of being scrutinized by the club's members. Acceptance or rejection by those members is often based on social status, demonstrated by how well the candidate handles himself at the table.

Dinner-table angst can be avoided by frequenting high-toned restaurants alone and asking the server how to eat a particular food, or waiting until other diners you may be with start eating and copying them. Keep in mind that sophisticated people got that way the same ways you will—either through trial and error, or with a mentor. Search the internet for an etiquette consultant in your area. Travel to find one if you must. These consultants are experts at grooming men to reach their next level of competency.

Artichoke

It is eaten with the fingers, one petal at a time. Dip the meaty end in the sauce and pull it through your slightly clenched lower teeth. Eat as much of the leaf as is edible, and then discard the petals in neat piles on the side of your plate. When you have eaten to the bottom of the choke, scrape off the prickly stamens with your knife and fork, then cut the heart into pieces; dip each piece into the sauce using your fork.

Asparagus

You may choose to eat short stalks with your fingers or cut long thin stalks with a knife and a fork, especially when they are limp. Dip the tips into sauce, and eat down until the spears become tough. Put any uneaten part of the branches back on the plate. In three-star (top) French restaurants, jumbo asparagus stalks are eaten with the left hand.

Bacon

It is eaten with the fingers if it is crisp. Limp, greasy bacon is eaten with a knife and a fork.

Beverages

Once a spoon has been used, it is not placed back on the table. If you're using a cup and saucer, lay the spoon on the saucer behind the cup handle. If drinking out of a mug, place the spoon on a nearby plate or napkin; if neither is available, ask for a side plate. The last resort is to place it on the table if it will not cause a stain.

Bread and rolls

They are eaten held in one hand. Break the bread into quarter-sized pieces. Take a small pat of butter from the butter plate, and put it on the edge of the bread plate, **not** directly on the bread. Butter and eat each piece individually.

Cake

Dry, non-sticky cake is eaten with the fingers. Moist, sticky, or custard-filled cake is eaten with a fork. Cake served with ice cream is eaten with a fork and a spoon. The fork pushes the portion onto the spoon, and the spoon is used to cut and to eat.

Canapés

They are cold appetizers of meats fish, vegetables, cheeses, or eggs served on bread or crackers. They are eaten with the fingers or utensils, depending on how they are served.

Candy

When wrapped candy is presented on a dish, remove the wrapped candy, fold the wrapping and place it on a plate. When taking candy from a box, remove the paper holder along with the candy. Never leave half-eaten candy in the box.

Caviar

Scoop the caviar from its serving bowl onto your plate with the spoon provided (use mother of pearl or glass, not stainless steel or silver as it will make the caviar taste metallic). Put about one teaspoon of the caviar on your plate. Spread the caviar on a cracker or with a toast point. Eat the toast with your left fingers.

Cheese

When cutting into cheese, be considerate of others and leave the platter nearly as neat as it was presented to you.
- Sliced cheese served with pie is eaten with a fork. If it is served on a tray with a toothpick, it is eaten with the fingers.
- Small pieces of a cracker are broken off and eaten with a piece of cheese. The rind of soft cheese is edible; the rind of hard cheese usually is not and is removed with a knife.
- The tip of a triangular wedge of soft cheese like Camembert is the best part. It's not nice to cut it off and take it for yourself.

Chicken, turkey, duck and chops

If you're outdoors, eat the pieces with your fingers. If you're indoors, eat it with your knife and fork until you reach near the bone. Excuse yourself to pick up the bone by saying, "This is so delicious. Do you mind if I pick this up?"

Clams and mussels

When served raw, clams are served detached on the half shell and seasoned with lemon wedges, pepper, or hot sauce. Hold the shell in the left hand, and pierce the flesh with a fork, then drink the remaining juice from the shell; or tip the entire contents directly into your mouth from the shell, and eat in one bite without making any noise. Place the shell on the side of the plate. Fried clams are served out of the shell as a finger food or eaten with a fork.

Corn on the cob

It should not be served at a formal dinner. Butter, season and eat only two rows at a time, not around the cob. Hold either with prongs or in both hands. Remove stuck bits of corn between your teeth away from the view of others.

Crab (See lobster.)

Crackers

Except at home, crackers are not crumbled into soup. At formal meals, if crackers are served with cheese, they are placed on the edge of the plate and eaten a bite at a time. If a plate is not provided, place the crackers on the table.

Doughnuts

Do not dunk in public.

Eggs

Place the pointed end of a soft-boiled egg down into the egg cup. Tap around the shell cap with the knife, and then slice it off. Place the cap on the plate. Eat directly from the shell with a spoon, or scoop the egg out into a dish and eat with a spoon.

Fish

If you ever order a small freshwater fish served whole, hold the fish fork in your left hand and the fish knife in your right hand and bone as follows:

- Hold the fish with your fork and use your knife to cut off the head behind the gills, then the tail, and put them to one side of the plate;
- Cut away a small edging of the fish along the stomach and the backbone; slit the body open with the notched tip of the fish knife;
- Use the fork and knife to lift away the top filet and lay it flat on the plate;
- The backbone will lie exposed and the cut-away filet will be free of bones;
- Slip the knife between the filet and the backbone;

- Lift away the backbone and put it next to the head and tail. The fish is ready to eat.

Fondue

Cheese sauce is served in a communal pot. Spear and dip cubed bread into the cheese sauce with the fondue fork, one per guest. Remove the bread cube from the fork with the front teeth only. Neither the lips nor the tongue ever touches the tines.

Hors d'oeuvres

When they are served on a toothpick from a tray, don't put your used toothpick back on the tray; put it in the container provided, which the server has in his other hand. If there isn't a container, place the toothpick in an ashtray or hold it until you can get rid of it.

Lobster

If served in its shell, it is cut in half and eaten with the fingers, a small fork, and lobster crackers. The chef may present it with the meat loosened from its shell. If not, hold the lobster over the plate with one hand; twist the large claws off and open them with a nutcracker. Remove the meat and eat with the lobster fork.

- Twist the smaller claws off and suck the meat from the cavity.

- Detach the tail from the body in a twisting motion.
- Break off the flippers at the small end of the tail with your fingers and pull out the meat with the fork.
- Split the tail and use the fork to lift the meat onto the plate.
- Crack the back shell and eat the meat with the fork.
- Eat the green liver (the tomalley) and the eggs (the roe) directly from the body with a fork.

Olives

They are eaten with the fingers when served as a garnish or as an hors d'oeuvre. If there is a pit, remove it with the fingers. Eat extra-large olives in two bites. In a cooked dish, eat them with a fork.

Oysters

The oyster season starts in September. They may be safely eaten in the months that contain the letter *R*. Oysters are served raw in their shells with lemon segments squeezed into the shell. Hold the shell in your left hand, spear the flesh with an oyster fork, and then drink the remaining liquids from the shell; or sip the entire contents directly into your mouth from the shell and eat.

Peas

Don't spear with a fork. The best way to eat them American style is to push them on the fork with a piece of roll or a knife. In European eating, they're squashed on the top of the fork. Peas are best not served at a formal dinner.

Pizza

If a small pizza is served as a separate first course at dinner, eat it with a knife and a fork. Otherwise, eat the slice with the hand as a finger food.

Salads

They are usually eaten with just a fork. Cut with a knife if necessary.

Sandwiches

Eat tea sandwiches and canapés with the fingers. Club sandwiches are cut into fourths and eaten with the fingers. Eat open-face sandwiches with a knife and a fork.

Sauce

Pierce a small piece of bread or roll with your fork, and then push the bread around in the sauce and eat it.

Sauces

May be poured over or beside meat. Dip a forkful of food at a time into the sauce.

Shrimp cocktail

Use a cocktail fork. Eat large shrimp in two bites. If the tails have been left on, hold the shrimp by the tail with the fingers, dip in sauce, take a bite, and place the tail on the under plate. For cooked shrimp, cut the tail off with a knife and eat the shrimp with a fork.

Snails

They are eaten directly from their shell, held by the left hand with tongs while the right hand removes the flesh with a snail fork. Dip in sauce and eat in one bite.

Soup

Scoop away from you so any drips fall into the bowl, and then sip noiselessly into the mouth from the **side** of the spoon. Don't blow on the soup, or any other food or drink, for that matter, that is too hot. Wait until it cools down, and eat from the sides of the bowl first so you don't burn your tongue. Crackers are not crumbled into the soup. They are eaten as an accompaniment. To get the last bit of liquid on the spoon, tip the bowl or plate **away from you.** Only a clear consommé, when served in a bowl with handles, may be drunk from the cup.

Spaghetti

Never cut spaghetti into pieces. Separate out three or four strands and twirl them with your fork held vertically. Sophisticated people do not use a spoon to eat spaghetti.

Sushi

It is usually eaten by hand, not with chopsticks. Only the fish part, not the rice, is dipped into soy sauce.

FRUIT

Eating fruit can be a social disaster for the uninitiated. It is best to practice eating some fruits in the privacy of your home. At a formal meal, use a knife and a fork to peel fruit, not your fingers.

Apricots, nectarines, peaches and plums

They are quartered and their stones left on the side of the plate. Peeled fruit is eaten cut side down so the juice can run onto the plate. Unpeeled fruit is eaten cut side up, so the skin can contain the juice.

Bananas

They are peeled and eaten with a knife and a fork when eaten at the table; otherwise, peel down as you go.

Cherries

They are eaten with the fingers at an informal meal. The pit is dropped into the palm of the hand and placed on the side of the plate.

Figs

Use a knife and a fork, if provided. Cut the fruit downward into quarters. Turn down the quarters to form a flower. Cut each quarter loose and eat with the hands, skins and all. Or, eat them with your hand, skin and all, in two or three bites.

Grapes

It is bad form to pick off individual grapes from the stem. Use grape scissors or your hands to break of a small clump, and eat each grape by hand.

Grapefruit

It is correctly served with the sections cut loose. If it isn't, return it to the kitchen to avoid squirting yourself and others. Eat the grapefruit with a spoon. Don't squeeze out any remaining juice in public.

Kumquats

Cut off the top end, and eat whole and with the hand.

Mangos

Slice off an oval-shaped slice of skin and fruit. Slice down the cut piece into a grid pattern. With both hands, bend the peel backward to force up the pulp into easy-to-eat cubes. You may also cut the cubes along the peel to remove from the skin, and eat with a fork. Repeat for each new slice. Or when no one is looking, peel it and eat it like a peach. Have plenty of napkins to sop up the mess.

Melons

They are served with a knife and a fork. Remove the rind by sliding the knife under the meat, and sectioning it. Eat the melon with the fork. If no fork is provided, use your fingers. Remove watermelon seeds into the cup of your hand and place them on the side of your dish.

Oranges and tangerines

They are peeled in a circular motion with a knife or with the fingers. Make sure to remove the pith, and then eat one segment at a time with the fingers.

Papayas

They are sliced in half lengthwise and eaten with a spoon. Squeeze lime over and enjoy.

Pineapple

It is eaten with a fork when it is served in quarters or in slices. If it is cubed, eat it with a spoon.

Odd Stuff

- Islamic and Indian cuisines — They are traditionally eaten with bread or lettuce leaves, and the fingers. Scoop up the food and eat. Always use the right hand when eating. For sanitary reasons, traditionally the left hand never touches food or the mouth.

- Double dipping is nasty. Once a chip or whatever has been bitten into, never reintroduce it into a communal bowl. The better form is to break the item into a bite-size piece, dip it, eat it, and begin again.

- Food that falls off your plate onto the table may be put back onto your plate with your fork or spoon, or your fingers when no one is looking.

- Don't saw your food; cut it, lift your knife, then cut it again, but no more than two or three times.

- Don't cut more than one piece of food at a time; our moms did that for us when we couldn't cut for ourselves.

- To get the last bit of sauce or gravy, break off one piece of bread at a time, pick the piece up with your fork, and dip it into the bowl.

- Eating from communal serving dishes is nasty and shouldn't be done.

- Picking your teeth at the table is vulgar. If you have food stuck in your teeth, try drinking water to dislodge it, or excuse yourself and go to the restroom to take care of the problem.

- If flatware is dirty or spotted, don't "clean" it on your napkin, ask the server to bring you a replacement. If you drop a piece, don't pick it up and place it on the table. Leave it and ask for another.

- When you are finished eating, don't scrape, stack, or push away your dishes. The proper placement of your flatware in the "I am finished" position on your plate will signal to the server that you are done.

- Don't eat with your fingers unless you are munching at a cocktail party or at a barbecue.

- To refuse foods or a beverage just say, "No, thank you." Don't turn your cup over or place your hand over the glass.

CHAPTER 4
ENTERTAINING FOR BUSINESS

In business, how prevalent are the graces, how detrimental is the want of them! The utility of them in negotiations are inconceivable.

—Lord Chesterfield

You may be fooling yourself if you are not worried about your ability to be at ease with fine dining at a five-star restaurant, or taking charge of hosting a business or a social dinner. If you wish to climb either the social or corporate ladder, you must have a veneer that is smooth and polished. You probably need help, because the truth is, there's no faking it. While it may be a jungle out there, animal house manners won't cut it for the office.

A tourist in New York asked a passerby "How can I get to Carnegie Hall?" The New Yorker replied, "You have to practice" and walked on. That's what you have to do: Practice, practice, practice in order to upgrade your image. On whom should you practice? Start with yourself, and then move on to a best friend, family members, business associates, and finally that special person.

HOSTING A BUSINESS LUNCHEON

Begin by frequenting several upscale restaurants. These establishments should reflect the image you wish to project about yourself. Learn their geography, layout, menu, where the best tables are, and the names of the servers. Develop a rapport with the wait staff and the maître d' (short for *maître d'hôtel,* or master of the hotel) and have them recognize you. This will all help to impress your business guests.

Treat guests in a restaurant the same as you would if you were inviting them to your home. It is your responsibility to take charge of every detail of the event, from picking up the phone and extending the invitation yourself, to paying the bill and the valet parking.

How to Choreograph a Meal

Extend the invitation to your guests at least one week before the meeting. Tell them the reason for the meeting, and where and when it will be. This is the time to ask if there are any dietary restrictions. If you make your invitation by phone, send a confirmation card to arrive two days before your meeting. This acts as a reminder in the event of an oversight. Verify your arrangements with the restaurant the day before the meeting.

Avoid any ambiguity as to who is paying by stating that you'd like to invite the person to lunch as *your guest*. Don't ask your guests where they want to eat. Keep in mind travel distance, their tastes and importance, then offer a choice of two restaurants with which you are familiar. The fewer people at the meeting, the more productive it will be. Invite others only if they are important to your agenda.

The Restaurant

Make reservations in your name as far in advance as possible. When booking the table, specify where you would like to sit. Learn the table numbers of the best locations, and request that table at the time you make your reservation. Never sit next to the kitchen, the restrooms, the supply station, or by mirrors (they are too distracting).

Prearrange the menu if time is an issue and if more than six people will be attending. If you will be entertaining at a restaurant with which you are unfamiliar, either ask to have a menu faxed or sent to you, or download it from the Internet. Learn the menu for possible suggestions. You never want to look unprepared.

Arrive early to allow yourself time to check the arrangements and the menu. Greet your guests in the lobby, not the bar. If there is no lobby, go to the table, and ask the maître d' to escort your guests to your table. Don't order a drink, munch on the breadsticks, or open your napkin once you've sat down. Your guest should see you sitting at an undisturbed table.

You can get more done with a one-on-one meeting. If you know that someone is always early, arrange with the captain to acknowledge your appointment with him or her for the scheduled time, and that you soon will be arriving. For a chronic latecomer, modify your time accordingly. It is courteous to wait half an hour after the scheduled time before you order or you decide to leave. If you choose to leave, it is appropriate to tip the server the price of a meal for having taken up a table from which he or she would have earned that day.

If there is no greeter, stand and wave your guests to your table. If the maître d' seats all of you, he or she will lead your guests and you follow. When seating yourself, you take the lead and your guests follow.

As in any situation, call the restaurant if you are going to be late by even a few minutes.

Being Seated

As the host, you decide the seating arrangements. Point out a chair for each guest and ask him or her to sit there. The most important guest gets the most desirable seat at the table. This may change. In general, seat your most important guest looking into the restaurant, but if your restaurant is noted for its view, seat that guest looking out. If your guests are late, state that you just sat down yourself.

Host and One Guest

When there are two of you at a meal, unless it is a booth, sit at a right angle to your guest. Sitting across from one another at a square table is considered an adversarial position. Seat a left-handed person to your left.

Host ▢
  Guest

Host and Two Guests

When hosting two guests, seat the more senior person across from you, and the more junior on your left if you are right-handed, or on your right if you are left-handed. If you seat them on either side of you, you will be moving your head back and forth as in watching a tennis match. If you have a co-host, sit at the head of the table with your co-host at the opposite end.

Host ▭ Guest 1
  Guest 2

Host with Co-host and Six Guests

When hosting multiple guests, sit at the head of the table with your co-host at the opposite end of the table. Seat the most important guest on your right; the second-most important guest is on your left. The third-and fourth-most important people are seated at your co-host's right and left, respectively. The guest ranked number five sits next to guest number one; the guest ranked as number six sits next to the guest ranked number two.

	Guest 2	Guest 6	Guest 3	
Host				Co-host
	Guest 1	Guest 5	Guest 4	

At the Table

Ask for a large table in a quiet corner if you think you may have to spread out papers. Don't make or take telephone calls at your table. This suggests to your guests that you didn't set aside a special time for them, and that they do not have your undivided attention. It is rude to other diners for you to talk on the telephone while you are eating. You got out of the office to escape those calls and to focus on your guest!

Once everyone is seated, it is your responsibility to give the silent signal that the meal may begin by placing your napkin on your lap. Smaller luncheon napkins are unfolded completely. Larger dinner napkins are left folded in half; keep the napkin on your lap, not across one knee, throughout the meal.

Offer your guests something to drink. "What are you having to drink?" is classier than "Do you want a drink?" If your guests order a beverage, you should also, even if you don't want one. It doesn't have to be alcoholic.

Make a recommendation of one or two main dishes. This should indicate a price range within your budget. Let guests order first if you don't have a prearranged menu. If they order salads, you should, too, so that they are not eating alone. Take a bite, and push the rest of the food around on your plate, if you must.

You are responsible for noticing that the food was prepared for your guests as they ordered it. If the food is cold or not cooked properly, send it back; if you need to reorder for yourself, select a different dish, but avoid making a scene or behaving badly. If you are unhappy with the service, excuse yourself and discuss it with the maître d' sufficiently away from others.

If you need to leave the table in the middle of the meal, put your napkin on the seat of your chair, not on the table. You want to leave the table looking as neat as possible; this is also a signal to the server that you will be returning, and not to take your plate away.

Getting Down to Business

Don't jump into your business until after the orders have been taken and the appetizers have been served. If you are hosting a luncheon, use the first ten minutes for "small talk." For a dinner, allow thirty minutes. This gives everyone a chance to relax and establish rapport.

Paying the Bill

When you invite a client to lunch, you pay. If the client suggests lunch, and you profit from the meeting, you still pay. Check ahead of time to ensure that the restaurant takes the credit card you are planning to use. If you frequent a particular restaurant, consider having your company open a house account for that establishment.

When hosting a lunch or dinner, the worldly businessman doesn't fuss with the check. There are sophisticated ways to handle paying the bill. You may give the captain your credit card ahead of time, and request that he ask the server to add 18 percent to the meal. The server knows he's going to get a little more tip, and hopefully will give you better service. The server runs your credit card ahead of time, and returns it and the receipt for you to sign at the table at the end of the meal.

You may also request that the receipt not be brought to your table. Arrange either to pick it up on your way out or have it sent to your office; or you may request that the bill be held at the captain's station. Excuse yourself as the meal is coming to a close, and go there to review and sign the slip and pick up your receipt.

If the slip is brought to your table, pick it up, and check the total without comment. Put the check *face down* on the tray in a folder with your card or money underneath.

To indicate the end of the meal, pick up your napkin and place it on the left side of your plate. Don't crumble it into a wad or refold it.

Odd Stuff

- The first time you meet someone should not be over dinner, unless your client is from out of town or has suggested it. It is considerate to include your out-of-town guest's spouse at the dinner, but in this case, bring along your spouse, or someone who can entertain the client's spouse while you are conducting business.

- Thank the maître d' with either a phone call, or write a note later that day. You will be remembered.

- You must dress and behave up to the level you wish to ascend.

HOSTING A BUSINESS DINNER AT HOME

If you will be hosting a business dinner at home, the rules are basically the same as for entertaining in a restaurant. Unless you have staff, it is best to engage a caterer to achieve the professional look you want to project. If there will be a bar, ask someone to mix the drinks. Contact a culinary school to find someone willing and able to coordinate the meal and act as server. Make sure your home is spotless. Order a floral centerpiece for the table. If you are single, ask someone to take the role of co-host. If you have children or pets, keep them out of the event.

CHAPTER 5
ALL YOU NEED TO KNOW ABOUT WINE (FOR NOW)

White meat, white wine; red meat, red wine.

—French proverb

Matching wines to food is not difficult once you realize that it's just putting two like things together, e.g., rich food calls for a rich wine, acidic food requires a high-acid wine. Daily, simple foods require simple wines. Hot weather calls for light wines, cool weather calls for something more substantial. There are three schools of thought on the subject of pairing.

Traditionalists. In the last few decades it has been difficult to find anyone, other than the wine connoisseur or quality chef, who pays strict attention to the harmony of wines and foods. For centuries, gastronomic experts have matched for us the foods and wines that grow in their own regions. *Wines match well with certain foods when the tastes are alike.* Exceptions always exist, but usually white, rosé, and sparkling wines are compatible with delicate foods, and red wines match well with rich, hearty food. It's the gray area of flavors that cause the greatest confusion. For instance, both red and white wine complement the light-colored meats like poultry and veal.

Neophytes. The neophyte chants the mantra of ordering any wine to suit your own palate. While I don't think it's necessary to be a slave to tradition, I do think this philosophy is a matter of sour grapes. Like an alien pouring catsup instead of chocolate over ice cream, the neophyte proclaims that uninformed choices are acceptable, and then convinces himself that anyone who believes differently is a snobbish purist.

Centrists. Happily, we are now encountering a new generation of sophisticated wine drinkers who are aware of the rules and are making informed choices. Once you know some basics, you can bend them in favor of the choice that will still give you balance, as when choosing a wine to be served with a highly flavored light-meat dish. In order for you to benefit from knowledge learned over years of trial and error, if you are a novice, you are probably better off following simple pairing techniques for now. You can strike out on your own later, as your tastes develop.

The rule of white wine with fish and red wine with beef and fowl is quite basic. Food and wine matching is an art; therefore, the blending of cooking ingredients and sauces must be taken into consideration when showing both at their best. This art is at the brink of disappearing simply because few take the time, or have the interest, to understand it. It's a lot classier to acquire wine sophistication by doing your homework. One woman I met bragged to her group of listeners that she drank nothing but Champagne. I remembered my manners and refrained from quipping back "How boring"!

There are wine drinkers who choose red wine for everything. Here is a short explanation of dyes and tannins. Red grapes can make white wine as well as red. If the juice of the grape is fermented without the red pigment in the skin, the wine stays white, regardless of the color of the grape. Tannin is an extract in the skin that serves as a preservative in wine, one of the reasons red wine ages longer than white wine. Tannins in red wine can leave a dry, chalky residue covering the teeth and gums, and are what make you pucker your lips. They can create an iodine flavor when mixed with fish oils—one of the reasons for avoiding drinking red wine with fish. Choosing a low-in-tannin, thin-skinned red grape is friendlier to the palate.

The wine you choose should be on an equal footing with the main dish, neither underpowered nor overwhelmed by it. Food and wine are equal partners, that when well-matched are better together than apart.

Choosing a wine that shares characteristics with the food is the more natural combination. Sometimes, contrasting the flavors is what's needed, and works well, once you know what you're doing.

Like a great symphony, a meal builds to a crescendo, with lighter dishes typically preceding heavier, richer dishes. Your wine choice should do the same.

If you are ordering wine as an aperitif, it's best to begin with lighter wines: brut sparkling wines; dry to fruity Riesling; Sauvignon Blanc and Beaujolais for those who drink only red wine.

APPETIZERS

Dry Sauvignon Blanc, Sémillon, Chenin Blanc, Pinot Blanc or Chardonnay (all without oak) are variety wines that can go with:

Green salads (without vinegar)
Vegetable salads
Tomato/mozzarella
Raw oysters/clams
Cured/smoked fish
Goat cheese

FISH

High-acid wines taken with fish will replace the lemon you would squeeze over it. The purpose of serving unoaked wine is to keep the lemon quality and to avoid the grape variety from competing with the food. Again, Beaujolais is the most appropriate red wine for those who prefer a red. The strong taste of some fish can support light-tannin red wines such as Pinot Noir and Barbera.

White wines *with* oak are better taken with dishes that have butter, cream or cheese sauces on them. A good choice is Chardonnay. Other good wine choices are Viognier, white Bordeaux, and dry Riesling from Austria. The following fish are often well paired with these wines:

Crab

Salmon

Sea bass

Lobster

Shrimp

Scallops

Monk fish

Coupled with dairy-based sauces, the wine qualities will be further complemented. These fish also pair well with red wines. Good choices that work are Pinot Noir, red Burgundy, or Barbera because they are low in tannin and will not overwhelm the dish.

WHITE MEATS

In chicken, veal, or pork served with butter, cream or cheese sauces, the dairy in the sauces complement oak-aged Chardonnay, Viognier, white Bordeaux, and dry Riesling. Grilling these white meats adds a smoky flavor that will also work well with white wines, with or without a sauce. Beaujolais, Pinot Noir, Barbera, Chianti, Sangiovese, and Zinfandel are the red wines of choice.

RED MEAT

A wide choice of red wines pairs with red meat. Remember that the longer the juice is left in the oak barrel with the skins and stems, the higher is the tannin content of the wine—which gives the wine "body." These big, red wines are for rich meat dishes of:

Beef
Lamb
Venison
Braised meats

Red Bordeaux, Cabernet Sauvignon, and Merlot shine with rich meat dishes. Barolo and Barbaresco, which tandem well with a simple grilled steak, and Syrah for lamb, are the wines of choice. Your white-wine selection should be able to stand up to meat dishes. Barrel-aged Chardonnay, Viognier, and Gewürztraminer should be your main choices.

Odd Stuff

- Although red wine is traditionally served with red meat, a chilled glass of white wine might be more suitable during the summer. A simple rule to help make summer dinners more enjoyable is to put your red wine in the refrigerator for ten minutes, as you take the whites out. In this time you can lower the temperature of red wine 10 degrees Fahrenheit or so and make it more enjoyable, especially on hot days. White wine at refrigeration temperature is too cold to fully enjoy the bouquet and needs to warm up a bit—approximately ten minutes before serving.

HOT AND SPICY

Spicy dishes like Indian or Thai curry are traditionally coupled with beer, so they have their own needs when coupled with wine. Wines that are medium-dry to sweet work well with them, because the residual sugar left in the wine coats the mouth and protects it from the heat in the dish. This is an example where sweet contrasts well with spicy. When coconut milk is added to Thai food, it also provides sweetness. Then choose a sweeter wine to complement the sweetness in the dish. Avoid wines that are high in alcohol, which only serve to make the dish seem hotter. Wines that go well are German Riesling, and French Vouvray or Gewürztraminer.

CHAPTER 6
THE ORDER OF WINE SERVICE

In vino veritas. (In wine there is truth.)

—Roman proverb

At a luncheon or for informal dining, one wine, either white or red, may be served, but it should be light and blend with all courses. Try to match some quality in the wine to a like quality in the food, e.g., pair an acidic Italian wine with tomato-based pastas or a full-bodied Syrah with rich pork or lamb. If one wine is served at a simple meal, it should complement the main course. When two wines are served, use these guidelines:

- Rosé first
- White before red
- Dry before sweet
- Light before full
- Young before old
- Acidic wines with acidic and salty dishes
- Sweeter wines with less sweet food

FORMAL DINING

While it is rare today to host a seven-course meal, the following courses are listed along with wine suggestions so that you can choose which among them you would like to serve, and as a guide for serving wine from an expanded repertoire.

Just as a multicourse dinner is started with a light course of an appetizer or soup, proceeds to heavier, richer dishes, and ends with a salad and dessert, your wine choices should reflect this as well. A very small serving of a citric sorbet is presented between the fourth and fifth courses to cleanse the palate. When I was a child, the first time my sister and I were presented with this refreshing *entremet*, we thought it was a puny serving of dessert. It takes time to become knowledgeable.

The sophisticate knows that in Europe the *entrée* is either a soup or appetizer, the *main meal* is either fish or meat, and that salad is served after the main meal. The order of courses is:

Appetizer
Light, dry
   Generally white, sherry, or sparkling

Soup
Light, dry
   Generally white Burgundy, sherry, or sparkling

Salad

No wine is served with a vinegar-based dressing because the acid content of the dressing would overpower the wine. If you wish, use a lemon dressing and a dry white.

Fish
Light, dry
Generally white, such as Pinot Blanc, Sémillon, Sylvaner, Gewürztraminer, or sparkling

Meat, light
Light red or white
Pinot Grigio

Meat, red
Medium red
Pinot Noir or Cabernet Sauvignon

Sorbet
No wine. It is served to "cleanse the palate."

Poultry
Medium red or white
Rioja or Barbera

Game
Medium, generally red
Pinot Noir or Cabernet Sauvignon

Cheese
> *Medium red or white*
>> Depending on the cheese

Dessert
> *Heavy sweet*
>> Madeira, Marsala, port, or Sauterne

Fruit
> Dessert wine

Coffee
> Liqueurs, cordials, brandy, and cognac

Chocolate
> Ruby port

INFORMAL DINING

Appetizer
> Serve a white wine.

Main course
> The food will determine the wine.

Dessert
> A sweet dessert wine

Coffee

In order to let guests circulate, coffee may be served in another room, but changing rooms can disrupt the mood of the evening. For an intimate party, it is satisfactory to serve coffee at the dinner table.

You do not have to serve an after-dinner drink. Serve one red wine or one white wine throughout the meal. Serve a sparkling white wine throughout the meal.

TYPES OF WINE

Aperitifs

Appetite is stimulated by effervescence and acidity in a wine, and inhibited by a sweeter one. At ancient Greek symposia, wine was diluted with water in the proportion of three parts water to two parts wine. That's why people could drink throughout the evening and still stay sober. A half-and-half mixture of wine and water was considered naughty. It has always been considered bad form to get drunk.

As far back as the Middle Ages, wine was served only during and after meals. Today, aperitifs are served before the meal to stimulate the appetite, because they do not overwhelm the taste buds with acid. An aperitif is a wine made by adding flavoring agents and brandy to boost its alcohol content, which ranges from 17 to 21 percent by volume. Some aperitifs taste bitter, while others are sweet. Vermouth has a sharp taste that complements cheese, caviar, nuts, and olives. Any white, light red, or dry rosé also may be used to whet the appetite. Bitters aid the digestion, and are served after the meal. The alcohol content is 45 to 49 percent. They are served in a shot glass with a side glass of ice water. Cream sherry is a sweet aperitif served later in the day when sweet foods, such as savories and jams, are served with afternoon tea.

Wines fortified with brandy have an alcohol content of 16 to 21 percent, and are served in their own specially designed, small-tulip-shaped glass. Dry fortified wines are served cool, about 55 degrees Fahrenheit, sweet wines, at approximately 50 degrees Fahrenheit.

Rosés

Thirst is quenched by a light wine, and so it is served first. If a heavier wine is drunk first, the light wine following it seems even thinner by comparison, and it cannot be appreciated in its own right. Rosés have a fruity taste, either dry, sweet, or in between. They tandem well in warm weather with both red meat and simpler prepared dishes made of chicken, veal, salmon, ham, vegetables, and fruit.

White Wines

White wine flavors range from sweet to dry. The flavor of a dry white wine can be lost in:

- Asian and South American dishes that are flavored with garlic, curry, or chili powder. These dishes pair better with beer, but are great with Chardonnay, Pinot Noir or Viognier.

- Green salad or antipasto. The acid in vinegary salad dressing and the acidity in white wine compete with one another and produce a bitter taste. For this reason, *white wine is not served with a salad with a vinegar dressing or antipasto course, unless it is balanced out with oil.*

- Acidic fruits such as lemons, oranges, and grapefruits overpower the flavor of a dry white wine, unless they are balanced out with oils.

- Overly oily fish such as sardines, anchovies, salmon, herring or mackerel.

- Ice cream.

- Chocolate. Sherry is an exception.

Red Wines

A Burgundy or Cabernet Sauvignon contains less than a fraction of sugar and complements foods served as the main course. The acidity of a red wine cuts the flavor of food with a high-fat content such as rich red meat, game, or duck, appetizers and light dishes made with chicken, fish, fowl, eggs, veal, and fruit. A dry wine doesn't follow a sweet dish, because it will taste bitter in comparison.

The bouquet of a wine is released when the wine is gently swirled in a half-filled glass. Bring the glass to your nose and take four or five short sniffs. Longer sniffs dull the sense of smell.

To pair wine with food, vintners use descriptions that identify the bouquet of the wine with nature:

Fruity

Refers to a bouquet and flavor that is similar to fruit. It does not mean sweet or grapey.

Earthy

Wines taste of minerals, such as clay and gravel; Bordeaux and Burgundy.

Grassy

Wine has the suggestion of grass or herbs; Sauvignon blanc and Soave, Orvieto.

Nutty
> Flavor taste similar to nuts, such as almonds; sherries, white Côtes-du-Rhone.

Vanilla
> Flavor comes from barrels of wood that contain vanillin, new oak barrels.

Oaky
> Describes a wine that has absorbed that flavor from the barrel.

Sparkling Wines

Wines that are grown in the Champagne district of France have the exclusive use of that name. A white table wine that undergoes a second fermentation to add carbon dioxide gas to produce bubbles is called sparkling. Effervescent wines made someplace other than in Champagne have this designation. Like Champagne, they can be served throughout the meal and can be either sweet or dry, and are food-friendly, in general. Dry sparkling wine is served as an aperitif before dinner and as a table wine to accompany a meal or a particular course. Sweet sparkling wine is served with dessert. Wines go from dry to sweet according to the amount of sugar that is added during the styling process.

Sparkling-wine names:

Extra-brut
> Brut in French means crude or unrefined, and is a term used to describe Champagne to which no sugar is added. It is the driest Champagne.

Brut
> Describes Champagne with less than 1.5 percent sugar. The taste is very dry.

Extra-sec
> *Sec* means *dry*, which in the wine world means not sweet. "Extra dry" is slightly sweeter than brut.

Sec
> For sparkling wines *sec* means a relatively sweet wine.

Demi-sec
> It means "half-dry" and is sweeter than *sec*.

Doux
> It is "sweet."

Dessert Wines

- If the wine isn't sweeter than the dessert, the wine will taste less sweet than it normally would.
- Sweet dessert wines, such as off-dry Rieslings and Sauternes, pair well with sweet desserts such as cake,

berries and fruit tart pastries. Port goes well with walnuts and most blue-veined cheese.

- Sweet foods are improved when the wine is sweeter than the dessert. Dessert wine goes well with foods that have a contrasting flavor and texture, such as blue-veined cheese, mild crackers, and salty nuts.

- Place dessert wine in the refrigerator for thirty minutes to three hours before serving it. Chill Champagne or sparkling wine for approximately one hour. In a freezer, chill white wine, rosé, and dessert wine for five to ten minutes, and sparkling wine ten to twenty minutes or until the bottle is cool to the touch.

After-Dinner Liqueurs

Liqueurs, cordials, brandy, and cognac are served after dinner to stimulate digestion after a multicourse meal. They may be sweet or bitter, and aromatic. Alcoholic content is from 20 to 55 percent. Because of the high alcohol content, they are served in small glasses.

Anisette

A very sweet, colorless, Italian licorice-flavored liqueur made from anise seeds. Served without ice. Ice water is served on the side and added per individual taste. The water turns the liqueur milky and cloudy.

Amaretto di Sarronno
　　Distilled from almond with an intense almond flavor.

Bénédictine
　　Sweet taste made from twenty-seven herbs and spices by French Benedictine monks.

Cherry Herring
　　Dark red, cherry-flavored from Denmark.

Cointreau
　　Colorless French orange-flavored blend from sweet and bitter orange peels.

Crème de Cacao
　　Sweet white or brownish color with a chocolate flavor.

Drambuie
　　Scotch-based made from malt whiskey, honey and a blend of herbs and spices.

Grand Marnier
　　Orange-flavored with cognac.

Irish Cream
　　A blend of whiskey, cream, and chocolate.

Kahlúa and Tia Maria
　　Coffee-flavored from Mexico.

Ouzo

Colorless, unsweetened licorice-flavor from Greece. One part Ouzo to two parts water, which is served on the side.

Pernod

Yellowish, licorice-flavored. When diluted with a little cold water, it will turn white.

CHAPTER 7
BOTTLES, CORKSCREWS, POURING, AND MORE

> Drink thy wine with a merry heart.
>
> —Ecclesiastes

There is no such thing as wasted knowledge. Nothing is more powerful than to be able to join in a discussion, or to stop an insufferable showoff, by matching him or her with your own stockpile of information. The following tidbits, while not easy to work into everyday conversation, will allow you to hold your own when the occasion arises.

BOTTLES

In general you can tell what's in a bottle of wine by its shape. A Bordeaux wine bottle is narrow, has straight sides, and predominant shoulders. This is because the shoulders help stop sediment from running into the glass. Typically, red Bordeaux wines are bottled in green glass. Most white Bordeaux wines are found in clear glass. A magnum bottle has the same basic shape, only larger. The Burgundy bottle has shallow, sloping shoulders and also can hold either red or white wine. Champagne and sparkling wine bottles are thick-walled and tall-necked. They have no shoulders because they have no sediment. The indentation at the bottom of the sparkling wine bottle is called a "punt." It helps disperse pressure and so prevents the bottle from blowing out at the bottom. A German Hock bottle resembles a white-wine bottle, but is brown. Vintage port, Madeira, and sherry use sturdy bottles with wide shoulders, and often have a large bulge in the neck to help capture sediment. U.S. wineries have no standards about wine bottle shapes, but tend to follow these guidelines.

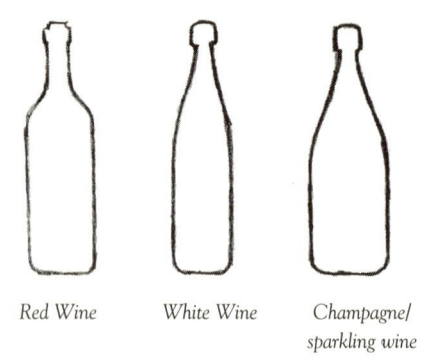

Red Wine   *White Wine*   *Champagne/ sparkling wine*

How to Open a Bottle of Still Wine

Spiral Corkscrew

- Hold the neck of the bottle for support and remove the foil with the blade of the corkscrew. Cut the foil to about a quarter-inch from the top or under the ridge on the neck of the bottle.
- Wipe the outside of the lip with a clean cloth to remove any dust or mold that may be underneath the capsule.
- Carefully insert the corkscrew three-fourths of the way into the center of the cork. This will help prevent pieces of cork from falling into the bottle.
- Turn the corkscrew, not the bottle.
- Avoid crumbling the cork by slowing and steadily easing it from the bottle with a turning motion.
- If cork bits are visible, wipe the inside and outside of the lip with the cloth to remove them.
- Before pouring the first glass, check if the cork left a deposit on the inside of the neck. If the cork breaks, push it into the bottle and hold it out of the way with a metal skewer while pouring. The wine may also be filtered through a clean piece of cheesecloth. A coffee filter works, too.

- Remove the foil far enough so that it will never be touched by the wine, which would cause the wine to pick up a metallic flavor.
- While holding the bottle over the glass, twist the bottle slightly after pouring to avoid spillage.

Single Lever

- Place the bottle on the table.
- Cut the capsule covering the cork to just below the ridge.
- Press the knife firmly against the glass as you cut all the way around.
- Remove the capsule, and wipe the lip of the bottle with a napkin to remove any mold, dust, or wine that has seeped.
- Insert the tip of the corkscrew slightly off center so that the "worm" will go down the center.
- Turn the corkscrew until the entire worm has entered the cork.
- Hook the lever onto the rim of the bottle.
- Using a rocking motion, raise the corkscrew until the cork is removed.

Pour table wine down the inside wall of a glass. Wine with a higher alcohol content is more viscous than low-alcohol wine, and produces shapes called tears or legs which appear on the inside wall of the glass.

◆ ◆ ◆

> In victory you deserve Champagne; in defeat you need it.
> —Napoleon Bonaparte

◆ ◆ ◆

How to Open a Bottle of Sparkling Wine

The neck of a bottle of wine is its weakest part. A corkscrew is not used to open a bottle of Champagne or sparkling wine because the insertion of a corkscrew in the cork compresses the cork against the neck of the bottle. The pressure created can cause the bottle to explode. Therefore, a cork with a cap is used. So instead:

- Remove the metal foil and twist the metal loop on the wire muzzle (the coiffe) to the left, and remove it.
- To avoid spillage, and to maintain the chill, wrap a napkin around the neck of the bottle.
- In order to transfer pressure away from the cork, hold the bottle at a 45-degree angle away from people and breakable objects.

- Hold the cork in place with your thumb over the cork while holding the bottle by the neck. With the other hand, gently turn and loosen the cork slowly. With the pressure gone, the cork should release with a soft pop. The less noise you make, the better.

So as not to be wasteful, be careful not to agitate the bottle. Despite what you may have seen in Hollywood movies, sparkling wine should not be allowed to explode out of the bottle and spill all over the floor. You want the CO_2 to stay in the liquid, since making the bubbles last longer contributes to the visual enjoyment as well. To avoid overly stimulating the bubbles and to maintain effervescence, pour the wine in a trickle immediately after opening the bottle. Pour a small amount of wine into a glass to let the foam settle, and then fill the glass.

THE CORK

Before cork was used, wine bottles were sealed with soft wood, wax or rags. To avoid unwanted material from spilling into a guest's glass, the hosts of old sampled the first-poured wine. The sophisticated person still follows this tradition. When you are hosting a dinner party, follow the ceremony of "pouring the cork." It gives a touch of class to the occasion, and announces that you are not embarrassed by what you know. After all of your guests are served, fill your own glass.

Contrary to popular belief, you do not sniff the cork—just inspect it to see if any wine has run up the sides. If it has, air might have got into the bottle. What you should do is smell your first-poured glass to tell if the wine is "off." The cork should be stained at the bottom and dry on top. A wine found to be tainted on opening is said to be "corked." It might have a pungent or moldy smell like wet cardboard and be brownish in color. A vinegary smell suggests sour wine. A dry cork indicates that air has entered the bottle and that the wine has gone bad. Pinch the end of the cork to determine the condition of the wine.

- Lay the cork next to the bottle so that your guests may see that it is wet.
- Don't pop the cork. Rock it slowly out of the bottle.
- If a piece of cork drops into your glass, scoop it out with a spoon or your knife tip, not your fingers. If the cork is completely mangled, just push it into the bottle, and then pour the wine through a coffee filter.

IN A RESTAURANT

If you are hosting an event at a restaurant, pinch the cork for moistness after the wine steward removes it. At a formal dinner the sommelier may remove and pinch the cork in the kitchen and leave it there. You now know the reasoning behind the traditional presentation of the bottle and the first tasting of the wine. Feel confident in performing this ceremony. Don't treat this ritual as an anachronism that has no meaning in today's eat-and-run society. Unless you are serving your guests a forgettable wine, give the ceremony its due. If you have ordered a memorable wine, treat it with dignity. Your knowledge will bring you respect.

- The server will present the bottle, label up, to show that you are getting what you ordered, and then pour a small amount of wine into your glass for you to taste. Check for color and clarity.

- Take this opportunity to check if the wine is at the right temperature. Smell it to ensure that it is unspoiled. If it is, immediately request another bottle.

- Take your time and ask questions if you are in doubt. Complaints after your acceptance are inappropriate.

- Once you have approved the wine, the server fills everyone's glass, starting with the women and ending with you, the host.

- The bottle will remain on the table. At a good restaurant, you should *never* have to pour your own wine.

POURING

When pouring wine, fill the glass about one-third full. This leaves enough space in the glass to allow your companions to gently swirl the wine without spilling and allow the aroma to float upward. Swirling allows you to better assess the bouquet, and softens a young, full-bodied red wine. There is about a one-ounce difference in the amount of wine poured into a white-wine glass and a red-wine glass. Because the red-wine glass is larger, fill it less than half. Restaurants will often fill it higher if wine is being ordered by the glass.

White wine and rosé

One-third full; three ounces

Red wine

One-half full; four ounces

Champagne

Three-fourths full; four ounces (Champagne and sparkling wine are not swirled because of their effervescence.)

Aromatic drinks

Two-thirds full or almost to the rim; aromatic drinks have a full bouquet that does not need to be released.

Brandy

One or two ounces are poured. Brandy glasses have a large bowl that creates a chamber for inhalation. Hold the brandy snifter in the palm of your hand, just below the nose in a still position. The heat from your hand will warm the brandy, releasing more bouquet and aroma. Swirling enhances the "nose," when the bouquet is first inhaled. Pass the glass under the nose several times, gently inhaling as the glass passes by. Don't inhale deeply because of the high alcohol content.

THE NUMBER OF SERVINGS PER BOTTLE

The ancient Greeks and Romans served diluted wine in order to prevent it from turning sour. Drunkenness was looked down upon and considered a lack of control. A moderate serving was considered three glasses. In that tradition, today's standard bottle of wine holds approximately six glasses, or enough for two people.

- A liter equals approximately thirty-four ounces, or a little more than one quart.
- A split is a quarter-size bottle and holds two glasses.
- A pint is one-half a standard bottle, or three glasses.
- A standard bottle (750 ml) serves each of six people a four-ounce drink.

- A magnum (1.5 liters) equals two bottles, or ten to twelve glasses.
- A jeroboam equals four Champagne bottles, or twenty-four glasses.

When buying wine for a party, calculate on the basis of five glasses of wine per standard bottle, rather than six. Before you buy, check that the liquor store will refund on unopened wine bottles, because this may be against the law in your state. A good rule is to keep extra bottles of white wine in the refrigerator, and an unopened bottle of red wine on the counter. Many guests do not drink red wine because the tannins upset their stomachs, and hosts avoid serving it because red wine is difficult to remove from tablecloths, carpeting and furniture fabric.

The number of courses served with the meal and the length of time your guests are seated at the dinner table determine the number of servings per bottle and the number of servings of wine you provide.

- Aperitifs are served before meals to whet the appetite; plan on five to six servings per bottle.
- When Champagne is served as an aperitif, allow two glasses per person.

- At a multicourse meal, allow for one glass of white wine and two glasses of red wine, or a minimum of three glasses of wine, for a total of twelve ounces per person.

- At a simple meal, allow two glasses, or eight ounces of wine per person.

- At luncheon, plan on one and a half glasses, or four to six ounces of wine per person.

- If Champagne is served as a main-meal wine, allow three glasses per person.

- When a dessert wine or Champagne is served with dessert, one glass per person is adequate. Based on a three-ounce serving, a bottle of dessert wine holds approximately eight glasses.

- If a liqueur or cordial is served after dessert and coffee, serve it in a small glass. Liqueur and cordial bottles hold approximately sixteen servings, or one and one-half ounces per person.

Odd Stuff

- If you are hosted at lunch by a woman, treat her the same as you would a male host, e.g., if the server shows you the wine list, direct him or her toward your hostess. Do the same for the bill. However, you still offer her your traditional civilities of standing when she does, and helping her into her seat, and later with her coat.

STORING WINE

Light Wine

We're told to store wine at room temperature. What experts tend not to mention is that for centuries, room temperature used to mean a room without heating or air conditioning, and could vary between 45 and 95 degrees Fahrenheit. Indoor weather control made it possible to live in homes without freezing or sweltering. If you don't have an underground cave to keep your wine stash at a constant temperature, the best place to store wine is in a cool, dark cellar, closet or buffet. The top shelf in your kitchen cabinets won't work because heat rises, and neither will your refrigerator, because both temperature extremes affect a wine's flavor. Changes in temperature also affect the flavor of wine; don't store it in a draft, near a heating vent, or in a room subject to temperature changes. Keep the bottle away from sunlight and low vibrations such as a washing machine or clothes dryer. White wines are best kept at a temperature between 49 and 56 degrees Fahrenheit. Rosés store best at temperatures between 49 and 54 degrees Fahrenheit.

Red Wine

Red wine is best protected against vaporization and loss of bouquet when it is served between 55 and 65 degrees Fahrenheit. Young and light reds can be stored on the cooler side. Aged mild and vintage wines do better in the upper range. To *chamber* a red wine stored in a cool place means to set it out and let the temperature rise slowly.

CHILLING WINE

In an emergency, you can quickly chill white wine, rosé, and dessert wine in a large bucket filled two-thirds with a mixture of half water and half ice. Don't omit the water, because ice alone will not chill the wine as quickly. Adding a large amount of rock salt to the water speeds the ice-melting process and increases the chill rate. Submerging a bottle up to the neck in water helps give it an even chill. To speed the chill rate even more, gently rotate the bottle to keep the wine in contact with the cool sides of the bottle. It takes about fifteen minutes to chill white, rosé, and dessert wine in an ice bucket.

To chill Champagne and sparkling wine in an ice bucket, follow the same directions, but eliminate the salt, which causes a too-rapid chill. This procedure will allow the Champagne and sparking wine to chill in approximately thirty to forty-five minutes.

As an emergency measure, white wine, rosé, and dessert wine may be chilled in your freezer for approximately five to ten minutes, and Champagne ten to twenty minutes, or until the bottles are cool to the touch. *Set a timer as a reminder not to have the bottle explode!*

Odd Stuff

- The best way to keep air from oxidizing wine, or to keep it from turning to vinegar after it has been opened, is to cork the bottle and put it in your refrigerator. If you have an empty half-bottle (375 ml) of wine, rinse it out well and save it in your pantry. The opening is the same size as a full bottle. When you don't finish a full bottle of wine, but less than half is left, pour it into the half-bottle and cork it. The less air that remains in a bottle, the longer your wine will last.

SERVING TEMPERATURE

The bouquet and flavor of light-bodied white, rosé, sparkling, and dessert wines are minimized when wines are stored in a refrigerator, but their tastes are improved when they are chilled for one-half hour to three hours and allowed to warm a bit before serving. Champagne or sparkling wine is chilled for approximately one hour before being served.

- Sparkling wines should be served chilled at 35 to 40 degrees Fahrenheit.
- White, rosé, and blush wines are best served chilled at 45 to 50 degrees Fahrenheit.
- Red wine is at its best at room temperature between 55 to 65 degrees Fahrenheit, unless it is served outside, in the summertime.
- Port, sherry, Madeira, Marsala, and vermouth should be stored at room temperature of 65 degrees Fahrenheit.

DECANTING

♦ ♦ ♦

Knowledge itself is power.

—Heresies

♦ ♦ ♦

The main reason to mention decanting here is to increase your knowledge-power base. Decanting is the process of pouring the wine from one bottle into another one—the decanter. Sediment results during the fermentation of red wine. The purpose of decanting wine is to prevent the sediment from the skins, seeds, and stems of the grapes in a mature bottle of wine from entering the glass. If sediment becomes mixed with the wine, the result can hide taste that has developed through the aging process, or can produce a bitter and unpleasant aftertaste. The second reason to decant is to aerate the wine. Air circulation allows volatile acids to escape, which helps to mellow the wine. The ritual of decanting during the eighteenth century included displaying the crystal bottle as beautiful, decorative objects on a sideboard.

How to Decant

You will need a candleholder, candle, paper napkin, corkscrew, and a carafe with a wide opening. One or two days before you serve your wine, stand the bottle upright, so that the sediment settles to the bottom. Don't shake the bottle when removing it from its rack. If the bottle has been disturbed, place the bottle in an upright position from several hours to one or two days.

- Remove the entire lead cap from the bottleneck with the corkscrew blade. Remove the cork, and wipe away any lead residue from the bottle opening. It's important to remove the cork in one piece and not shake up the bottle.
- Wipe the bottle opening with a paper napkin.

- Hold the neck of the bottle over a candle (a flashlight works, too) and slowly decant the wine into the carafe. The flame allows you to see what you are pouring and how close the deposits are to the opening.

- Touch together the openings of the decanter and the bottle. When the sediment nears the neck of the bottle, stop decanting so that you are not pouring any deposit into the decanter.

- Or, decant the wine into a funnel lined with a coffee-filter paper.

The practice of decanting was replaced in the nineteenth century when wine bottles themselves were considered a decoration, and were placed directly on a formally set table. The butler, originally known as the bottler, carefully removed the bottle from its storage place, holding it in the same position as it was stored. He held the bottle in his hand and faced the label toward the guests in order for them to see the vintage. The bottle was returned to the kitchen, and a decanter was not used.

SERVING WINE AT DINNER

Formal Service

Today when setting an elegant table, you may either leave the wine bottle on the table (for your guests to admire and to comment on the wine they are enjoying) or you may choose to impress your friends by decanting the wine, which you pour from your handsome vessel.

The best way to use a pair of decanters is to put one for red wine and one for white at opposite ends of the table, letting co-hosts serve guests who are sitting near them. A guest may refill his or her own glass by first asking the host, "May I?" to which the gracious host always agrees.

Informal Service

At an informal dinner, wine is left in its original bottle or decanted, depending on the preference of the host. Decanting can be a way to hide a less-than-impressive vintage year. Sometimes a deceptive host will place an inferior wine into an elegant decanter so that guests cannot see the original bottle's label, but for the most part, an inferior wine's odor and taste will speak for itself, and cannot be hidden.

White and rosé wines seldom contain sediment, and do not need to be decanted (except for informal service from a carafe). Champagne and sparkling wine are never decanted because they rapidly lose effervescence during the pouring process.

Odd Stuff

- When sitting down at dinner, pour for others who are seated next to you before refilling your own glass. It is boorish to fill your own glasses at a party and not those next to you, or to begin drinking before some food has been eaten to "line the stomach."

- Remember that glasses are not filled more than two-thirds to the brim. Gulping your drink or being drunk signals lack of class. If you've been eating, wipe your mouth before you begin to drink so that others are spared having to see a smeared glass.

- Serve your company starting with the guest on your right, and continue in a counterclockwise direction.

- Serve yourself last.

APPENDIX A
FOOD AND WINE PAIRING

Use this wine and food guide as a quick aid as you're going out the door for your next wine purchase or dinner.

GO-WITH-EVERYTHING WINE

It's easy to remember that "Champagne goes with everything"! There is a large selection of wines, including Italian Asti Spumante, and American sparkling wines that go under the umbrella of "Champagne," so that you do not have to pay for an expensive French wine. A dry or brut sparkling wine will serve the purpose. The following list is a quick reference for other go-with-everything wines. You probably already know Chianti and Merlot, so just add a few more names to your list and make a big impression. These wines have *not* been noted on the Food and Wine Pairing Chart on the following pages.

RED	**WHITE**	**SPARKING**
Beaujolais	Chardonnay	Asti Spumante (Italy)
Chianti	Gewürztraminer	Champagne
Dolcetto	Saké	Sparkling Burgundy
Gamay	Sauterne	
Merlot	Sémillon	
	Sylvaner	

Food and Wine Pairing Chart

The wine choices in this chart have been kept to a minimum, so that you can increase your ordering repertoire, build an impressive wine collection, and demonstrate an aura of sophistication, and still not spend a fortune. Some choices are out of the ordinary. Just remember, it is probably best to order and buy a wine from the country associated with the food origin. If you don't recognize the names of some of the foods listed, or have never tasted some of them, it is imperative that you begin educating yourself immediately, or risk looking as though you just fell off the turnip truck. Go to restaurants and start ordering them. All of them would be instantly recognized by a man of culture.

If there is someone in your group who is a wine aficionado, don't hesitate to defer to him or her for suggestions. It will make your job easier, and give recognition to the "expert."

L = Light
R = Red
W = White

S = Sweet
D = Dry
M = Medium

	Color	Taste	Country	Type
Aperitifs	W	S	France	Sauternes
	R/W	S	Italy	Vermouth
	Amber	D	Spain	Sherry
	R	S	United States, Portugal	Port (o)
Appetizers	W	D	United States	Pinot Blanc
	W	M	Germany	Riesling
	W	D	Italy	Soave
	W	D	Spain	Rioja
Rich	W	D	Various	Chardonnay
Bagels and lox	W	D	France	Chablis
	R	D	United States	Pinot Noir
Baked beans	R	D	California	Zinfandel

APPENDIX A 139

	Color	Taste	Country	Type
Beef				
barbecued	R	D	Australia	Shiraz
	R	D	California	Zinfandel
meat loaf	R	D	California	Cabernet Sauvignon / Zinfandel / Pinot Noir
simple preparation	R	D	France	Sauvignon Blanc
	R	D	California	Cabernet Sauvignon
	R	D	Italy	Bardolino
	R	D	Spain	Rioja
	R	D	Italy	Valpolicella
	R	M	France	Pinot Noir
pot pie	R	D	California	Cabernet Sauvignon
	R	D	Italy	Bardolino
pot roast	R	D	Spain	Rioja
	R	D	France	Sauvignon Blanc
	R	D	Various	Cabernet Sauvignon
steak	R	D	Italy	Bardolino
	R	D	Australia	Shiraz
	R	D	Spain	Rioja

	Color	Taste	Country	Type
stroganoff	Rosé	D	France	Tavel
Buffet, cold	Rosé	L	France	Tavel
	Rosé	L	California	Zinfandel
Candy	W	S	France	Vouvray
Canapés	W	M/D	Germany	Riesling
	W	D	Italy	Soave
	W	D	Spain	Rioja
	W	D	France	Chablis
Carpaccio	R	D	Italy	Sangiovese
Casseroles meat	R	D	Australia	Shiraz
Caviar	W	D	Italy	Pinot Grigio
	W	D	Various	Riesling

	Color	Taste	Country (or State)	Type
Chicken				
cold	W	D	California	Pinot Blanc
	W	M/D	Germany	Riesling
	W	D	Italy	Soave
with gravy	W	M/D	California, France	Sauvignon Blanc
pot pie	W	D or Semisweet	Italy	Orvieto
roast	R	D	United States	Pinot Noir
Southern fried	R	D	Australia	Shiraz
Chili con carne	R	D	Australia	Shiraz
	R	D	California	Zinfandel
Chinese food	W	D	California, France	Chenin Blanc / Chardonnay
Cold cuts	R	M	Various	Pinot Noir
	R	D	Italy	Barbera
Clam chowder	W	D	France	Riesling
Clams / oysters	W	D	California	Pinot Blanc

142 FOR MEN ONLY

	Color	Taste	Country	Type
Coffee	Liqueurs, cordials, brandy, and cognac		United States, Portugal	Port(o)
Crab				
Alaskan King	W	D	California	Chardonnay
Crêpes	W	D	France	Pinot Blanc
Desserts				
cakes/pastries	R	S/M	United States, Portugal	Port(o)
light	W	S	Italy	Pinot Grigio
	W	S	Germany	Riesling
cheesecake	R	S	California	Cabernet Sauvignon
	W	S/M	France	Sauternes
	W	M/D	Germany	Riesling
chocolate	R	S	United States, Portugal	Port(o)
crème brûlée	W	S	France	Sauternes
	W	S	Portugal	Madeira
Sorbet	Brandy	D	France	Cognac

APPENDIX A 143

	Color	Taste	Country	Type
Duck				
roast	R	D	Various	Cabernet Sauvignon
	R	D	Italy	Bardolino
	R	D	California	Zinfandel
Egg dishes				
Benedict	W	M	Various	Riesling
	Rosé	D	California	Pinot Noir
Fish				
barbecued	Rosé	M/Sw	France	Pinot Rosé
poached	W	D	Various	Chablis
in sauce	W	D	Various	Chardonnay
	W	M/D	Germany	Chenin Blanc
	W	M/D	Italy	Pinot Grigio
fried	W	M/D	Germany	Chenin Blanc
grilled	Rosé	D	Various	Cabernet Sauvignon
	W	D/M	Various	Chardonnay
Fondue				
cheese	W	D	California	Chardonnay
meat	R	D	Australia	Shiraz

	Color	Taste	Country	Type
Fruit				
fresh	W	S	France	Vouvray
light dessert	W	S	Various	Riesling
soufflés	W	S	Germany	Riesling
Game birds	R	D	California	Syrah
	R	D	Italy	Barolo
	R	D	Spain	Rioja
	R	D	France	Cabernet Sauvignon
Halibut				
grilled	W	D/M	Various	Chardonnay
in sauce	W	S	California, France	Sauvignon Blanc
Ham and eggs	Rosé	D	United States	Pinot Noir
	W	D	Various	Riesling
baked/boiled	W	D	Various	Riesling
	W	M/D	France	Vouvray
	W	M/D	Italy	Orvieto
	W	M/D	California	Chardonnay
Hamburgers	R	D	California	Cabernet Sauvignon / Zinfandel
	R	D	Australia	Shiraz

APPENDIX A 145

	Color	Taste	Country	Type
Hors d'oeuvres vegetable tray	W	D	France, Italy, California	Pinot Blanc
Indian food	W	D	Various	Chardonnay
	W	D	California, France	Chenin Blanc
	R	D	Italy	Bardolino
Japanese food	Rice	M	Japan	Saké
	W	D	Various	Riesling
Kabobs grilled	R	D	Various	Pinot Noir
lamb	R	D	Italy	Bardolino
	R	D	Spain	Cabernet Sauvignon
	R	M	Various	Syrah
	R	D	France	Bordeaux
Liver beef	R	D	Various	Pinot Noir
goose	W	D	California, France	Sauvignon Blanc

	Color	Taste	Country	Type
Lobster	W	D	California	Chardonnay
w/ cream sauce	W	M/D	Italy	Orvieto
Macaroni and cheese				
	W	M/D	California	Sauvignon Blanc
	W	D	Italy	Soave
	W	M/D	France	Vouvray
Melon	R	Fort.	Spain	Sherry / Madeira
	W	S	France	Sauternes
	Brown	Liq.	France	Cognac
Mussels	W	D/M	Various	Chardonnay
	W	D	France, Italy, California	Pinot Blanc (Bianco)
Nuts	W	Fort.	United States, Portugal	Port (o)
	R	Fort.	Spain	Amontillado / Madeira
	W	Liq.	Greece	Ouzo
	W	S	France	Vouvray
Omelet				
cheese	W	M/D	France, California	Chenin Blanc
	W	D	France, Italy, California	Pinot Blanc (Bianco)

	Color	Taste	Country	Type
Oysters	W	D	France, Italy, California	Pinot Blanc (Bianco)
	R	D	Spain	Rioja
	R	D	Various	Riesling
	W	D	Italy	Soave
Pancakes	Sparkling	S/M		
Pasta				
fettuccini Alfredo	W	D	Italy	Soave
lasagna	R	D	Italy	Barbera
ravioli	W	D	Italy	Pinot Grigio
Paté de foie gras	Brandy	Bwn	France	Cognac
	W	S	France	Sauternes
	R	M	Various	Cabernet Sauvignon
	W	D	France	Tokay
Picnic foods	Rosé	M	California	Zinfandel

148 FOR MEN ONLY

	Color	Taste	Country	Type
Pizza	R	D	Italy	Barbera
	R	D	California	Zinfandel
Pork				
cutlets	R	D	Italy	Barbera
	W	D	Italy	Pinot Grigio
chops	R	D	Various	Syrah
roast	R	D	California	Syrah
	W	M/D	California	Sauvignon Blanc
	W	D	Various	Riesling
	W	M/D	Germany	Chenin Blanc
Prosciutto	R	D	Italy	Barbera
	W	S	United States	Zinfandel
Quiche Lorraine	W	D	Italy	Pinot Grigio
	W	D	Various	Riesling
Rice (Risotto)				
Milanese	W	D	Italy	Pinot Grigio / Soave
Parmigiana	R	D	Italy	Barbera
mushroom	W	D	Italy	Pinot Grigio

APPENDIX A 149

	Color	Taste	Country	Type
Salad (None if there is a vinegar base)				
chef's	W	D	Italy	Soave
seafood	W	D	Italy	Soave
tomato	R	D	Italy	Barbera
tuna	Rosé	D	France	Sauvignon Blanc
Salmon				
	R	D	Italy	Bardolino
	R	D	California	Pinot Noir
	R	D	France	Burgundy
cold	W	D	California	Sauvignon Blanc
smoked	W	D	Various	Riesling
	W	D	France	Vouvray
Sausages	W	D	Various	Riesling
Sardines	W	D	Italy	Orvieto
Sauce				
Alfredo	R	D	Italy	Valpolicella / Barbera
butter	W	M/D	France	Vouvray / Chardonnay
pesto	R	D	Italy	Barbera
	W	D	Italy	Soave

150 FOR MEN ONLY

	Color	Taste	Country	Type
tomato	R	D	Italy	Barbera
	W	D	California	Sauvignon Blanc
vinaigrette	W	D	California	Sauvignon Blanc
	W	D	Italy	Pinot Grigio
white	W	D	Various	Chardonnay
Seafood				
w/cream sauce	W	M/D	California, France	Sauvignon Blanc
w/tropical	W	D	France	Viognier
flavors w/wine	R/W	M/D	France	Sauvignon Blanc
Scallops	W	D	Italy	Pinot Grigio
	W	D	France	Sauvignon Blanc
Shellfish	W	D	France	Sauvignon Blanc
	W	D	Various	Riesling
Shrimp	W	D	Various	Chardonnay
cocktail	W	D	California	Sauvignon Blanc
	W	D	Various	Riesling
curried	W	D	Various	Chardonnay
	W	D	France	Sauvignon Blanc

APPENDIX A

	Color	Taste	Country	Type
Soufflés				
w/cheese	W	D/M	France, Germany	Sylvaner
spinach	W	D	United States	Chardonnay
Soup (Wine, other than sherry, is not usually served with soup.)				
bisques	W	M/D	California	Sauvignon Blanc
	W	M/D	Germany	Chenin Blanc
clear	W	D	Spain	Amontillado
cream	W	M/D	France	Sauvignon Blanc / Vouvray
	W	M/D	Germany	Chenin Blanc
	W	M	Italy, California, France	Barbera / Sauvignon Blanc
rich	W	D	Various	Riesling
Stews				
simple or	R	D	California	Cabernet Sauvignon
casseroles	R	D	Australia	Shiraz
	R	D	France	Sauvignon Blanc
lamb, pork,	W	D	Various	Riesling
veal	R	D	Various	Syrah
	W	D	Various	Chardonnay

152 FOR MEN ONLY

	Color	Taste	Country	Type
Sushi	Rice	M	Japan	Saké
	W	D	Various	Riesling
Taco, beef	R	D	California	Zinfandel
	W	D	California	Riesling
Tuna	W	M	Italy	Barbera
Trout	W	D	Various	Riesling
Turkey				
cold	W	D	California	Pinot Blanc
	W	D	Italy	Soave
hot with gravy	R	D	California	Pinot Noir
	W	M/D	Italy	Orvieto
roast	W	D	Various	Chardonnay
	W	D	California, France	Sauvignon Blanc / Gewürztraminer
Veal	W	D	Various	Riesling
	R	M	Various	Pinot Noir
	R	M	Various	Cabernet Sauvignon

	Color	Taste	Country	Type
cold	W	M/D	California	Sauvignon Blanc
Parmigiana	W	M/D	Italy	Pinot Grigio
	W	M/D	Italy	Orvieto
Scaloppine	R	D	Italy	Barbera
w/ wine sauces	R	D	Spain	Rioja
Vegetables				
eggplant				
Parmigiana	R	D	Italy	Valpolicella
raw	R	D	Italy	Bardolino

APPENDIX B
CHEESE, FRUIT, CHOCOLATE, AND DESSERT

If you choose to serve cheese, the wine you select depends on the type of cheese you are eating. For a fresh goat cheese, Sauvignon Blanc is a classic choice. Soft cheeses go best with Chardonnay, both white and red Burgundy, Barbera, or Chianti. Rich, strong cheeses call for the richer flavors of the same red wines you would be having with your meat dishes. Sweet port is a good contrast to the salt of a cheese.

CHEESE	WINE
Soft	
Ripened	Pinot Noir, Gewürztraminer
Mild	Pinot Noir
Asiago d'Allevo	Oaked Chardonnay
Baby Bel	Gamay
Beaufort	Oaked Chardonnay
Brie	Full Chardonnay
Camembert	Bordeaux
Cheddar (Farmhouse)	Riesling, Gewürztraminer, Sémillon
Chèvre (Goat)	Pinot Noir / Sauvignon Blanc

Danish Blue	Schnapps, Sauternes
Edam	Chardonnay, Orvieto, Syrah, Zinfandel
Feta	Ouzo, Chardonnay
Fontina	Barola, Barbaresco
Gorgonzola	Barolo, Pinot Grigio. Port
Gouda	Chardonnay, Viognier, Pinot Gris
Gruyère	Sauvignon Blanc
Leicester	Pinot Noir
Manchego	Sherry
Monterey Jack	New World Chardonnay
Mozzarella	Orvieto, Soave, Pinot Grigio
Muenster	Gewürztraminer
Parmigiana-Reggiano	Barolo, Barbaresco
Roquefort	Sauternes, Port
Saga Blue	Riesling
Taleggio	Soave, Chianti
Tilsit	Gewürztraminer

Mild

Cream	Pinot Noir
Gouda	Cabernet, Tavel, Rosé
Edam	Pinot Noir, Beaujolais
Fontina	Barbaresco, Tavel, Rosé

Medium Strong

Alsatian	Bordeaux, Rioja, Beaujolais, Bardolino, Claret
Bel Paese	Light Chardonnay, Barbera
Camembert	Red Bordeaux, Rioja, Merlot

Feta	Ouzo
Monterey Jack	Chardonnay
Muenster	Gewürztraminer, Cabernet Sauvignon, Barbera, Bardolino, Graves
Provolone	Chianti, Dolcetto, Bardolino

Strong

Cheddar (English)	Chardonnay
Goat	Riesling, Gamay, Sémillon
Gorgonzola	Chianti
Parmesan	Barolo
Roquefort	Madeira, Syrah, Sherry, Sauternes
Stilton	Port, Sauterne, Rioja, Pinot Noir
Swiss	Bardolino

FRESH FRUIT

Fruits that are high in acid can make wines taste thin and metallic. In general, drink sweet white wine, especially sparkling with acidic fruits, whether they are in a salad, or as part of a dessert. The fruit should never be sweeter than the wine, or the wine will taste sour.

CHOCOLATE

As a general rule, white wine does not pair well with chocolate. A suitable match for this ever popular *bonne bouche* is sparkling wines, which can always hold their own with any rich dessert. Cabernet Sauvignon also matches well. Milk or dark chocolate calls for richer wines like Hungarian *Tokaji*. An unusual match is port, which goes well with most chocolate desserts or with chocolate alone. Memorize a few unusual wines, and you will impress everyone!

DESSERT

With dessert, your wine needs to be at least as sweet, if not sweeter, than the dessert itself. If it isn't, the dessert will make the wine seem tart, because of the acidity in the wine. With fruit tarts, you can impress everyone with your choice of a Moscato d'Asti, which is a light, sweet wine from Italy. Or drink the standbys Sauternes, Sémillon, or Rieslings, which work equally as well with vanilla, caramel, white chocolate, or crème brûlée. In Italy, a classic dessert combination is to dip almond biscotti into *Vino Santo*, which is a dessert wine with similar nutty characteristics.

APPENDIX C
INDEX OF WINE AND SPIRIT TERMS

It is better to remain silent and be thought stupid than to speak and remove all doubt.

—Confucius

It's important to be able to recognize certain terms when others are speaking. Knowing things is a bona fide way to attract the things you want to yourself.

Acidic:	A sour taste in the mouth.
Aroma:	The naturally produced fragrance of the grape. It lessens with fermentation, and with an aged wine is replaced by bouquet.
Astringent:	A puckering sensation in the mouth given to the wine by its tannins.
Balance:	The harmony of flavors as acid against sweetness; fruit flavor against wood, and tannic alcohol against flavor.
Big:	A high degree of alcohol, color, and acidity making a full and flavorful body.
Body:	Fullness and richness in the mouth caused by the alcohol, glycerin, and sugar in a wine.
Bouquet:	The fragrance produced when a bottle is opened, caused by fermentation and aging. It develops further after the wine is in the glass.

Brandy:	A spirit distilled from wine or fermented fruit juice.
Brut:	The driest of the sparkling wines.
Carafe:	A flared-lipped pitcher used to serve wine; also a crystal flask for the decanting of old red wines that contain sediment.
Chamber:	To bring out a red wine stored in a cool place and to let the temperature rise slowly.
Clarified:	A wine that has been filtered.
Cloying:	Too much sweetness and not enough acidity.
Coiffe:	The wire muzzle covering the cork on a bottle of sparkling wine.
Crisp:	Tastes dry; acid and tannins are pronounced.
Cru:	Literally, "grown." The area where the wine is grown.
Cuvée:	Refers to the first juice to flow from the press, a wine produced under a particular set of conditions or to a particular batch of wine.
Decant:	To pour off liquid from a bottle without disturbing the sediment in it.
Demi-sec:	Literally, "half dry." Used to describe the taste of sweet sparking wines.
Dry:	Not sweet.
Doux:	Sweet. Describes the taste of sparking wines.
Earthy:	The taste of soil in wine.
Estate bottled:	Indicates that a bottle of wine was supervised by the vintner from the field to the bottle.
Fermentation:	The process of converting sugar into alcohol by the introduction of yeast.

Frapper:	Literally "to chill." To cool warm beverages in an ice bucket.
Finesse:	A term designating refinement and class of a superior wine.
Finish:	The taste in the mouth after drinking the wine. The longer the aftertaste, the better is the wine.
Fortified:	A wine whose strength has been increased by the addition of alcohol during or after fermentation.
Full:	Having body and color; in wines that are high in alcohol, sugar, and extracts.
Jeroboam:	Equals four Champagne bottles, or twenty-four glasses.
Late harvest:	Refers to a wine made from overripe grapes with high sugar content.
Lees:	The sediment (dregs) of dead yeast cells and proteins left after fermentation.
Legs:	The streams of wine left on a glass after the glass has been swirled.
Liter:	Equals approximately thirty-four ounces, or a little more than one quart.
Magnum:	A large wine bottle, holding approximately fifty-two ounces.
Nose:	The combination of aroma and bouquet in the glass when the wine is smelled.
Powerful:	A robust, substantive red or a full white wine.
Punt:	The indentation at the bottom of a bottle of sparkling wine.

Sec: Literally "dry." All the sugar in the wine has been converted to alcohol during fermentation.

Sparkling: The generic term for an effervescent table wine. The name *Champagne* can be used only for grapes actually grown in the Champagne region of France.

Split: An eight-ounce bottle of sparkling wine. It's convenient for two people who wish to have just one glass of sparkling wine each.

Tannin: The binding acid from the skins, seeds, and wooden casks, which causes a puckering sensation in the mouth. It helps preserve quality wines, and adds to its complexity. Aging in the bottle softens a tannic wine.

Young: A recently bottled wine.

Varietal: Refers to a wine named after a grape from which it is made, with a minimum of 75 percent of the named grape used. A variety of grape reflects the soil and climate, often within a micro distance of another grape. It's the same grape, only different.

APPENDIX D
WINE AND SPIRIT PRONUNCIATION GUIDE

> It is better to remain silent and be thought stupid
> than to speak and remove all doubt.
>
> —Confucius

Those in the know will know that you're bluffing if you don't get the pronunciation correct. This is an extended pronunciation guide for when you branch out.

Legend

M = Medium
R = Red
S = Sweet
Sp = Sparkling
W = White

Temperature

C = Room temperature
CC = Slightly chilled
CCC – Cold
F = Fahrenheit

* Pairs with all foods

Name	Pronunciation	Type	Color	Taste	Serving Temp.
A					
Amontillado	ah-mohn-tee-YAH-do	Sherry	Amber	D	CC
Anisette	ah-nee-zet	Liqueur	W	Aniseed	C
*Asti Spumante	ahs-tee-spoo-MAHN-teh	Sparkling	W	S	CCC
B					
Barbaresco	bar-bah-REHZ-co	Table	R	D	C
Barolo	bah-ROH-low	Table	R	D	C
*Beaujolais	boh-zhoe-lay	Table	R	D	C or CC
Bitters		Spirit	Reddish	Bitter	C
Bordeaux Blanc	bor-doh-blah(n)	Table	W	D	CCC
Bordeaux Rouge	bor-doh roozh)	Table	R	D	C
Brandy	BRAN-dee	Fruit spirit	Amber	D, fruit	C
C					
Cabernet Sauvignon	kay-behr-nay soh-vee-nyoh	Table	R	D	C
Campari	kahm-PAR-ee	Aperitif	R	Bitter	CCC
Chablis	shah-blee	Table	W	D	CCC
*Champagne	shah(m)-pah-nye	Sparkling	W, Light	D to S	CCC
Chardonnay	shahr-doh-NAY	Table or Sp	W	D	CCC
Châteauneuf-du-Pape	shah-toh-nuf-dew-pop	Table	R	D	C
Chenin Blanc	sheh-neen-blah (n)	Table	W	M/D	CC

164   FOR MEN ONLY

Name	Pronunciation	Type	Color	Taste	Serving Temp.
*Chianti	kee-AHN-tee	Table	R	D	C
Cognac	koh-nyahk	Brandy	Brown	D	CC
D					
*Dolcetto	dol-CHET-oh	Table or Sp	R	D or S	C or CCC
*Drambuie	dram-BOO-EE	Aperitif	R or W	S	CC
G					
*Gamay	Gah-maye	Table	R	D	CC
*Gewürztraminer	geh-VURTZ-tra-mee-ner	Table	W	D	CCC
Grand Marnier	grah(n) mahr-nyay	Liqueur	Orange	S, orange	C
Graves	grahv	Table	R or W	D	C or CCC
H					
Hermitage	ehr-mee-tahzh	Table	R or W	D	C or CCC
J					
Johannisberg Riesling	yoh-hahn-is-behrk REES-ling	Table	W	M/D	CCC
K					
Kahlúa	kah-LOO-ah	Liqueur	Brown	S, coffee	C
Kirsch	keersh	Brandy	W	D, cherry	CCC

APPENDIX D 165

Name	Pronunciation	Type	Color	Taste	Serving Temp.
M					
Médoc	may-dohk	Table	R	D	C
*Merlot	mehr-LOH	Table	R	D	C
Meursault	mehr-soh	Table	W	D	CCC
Muscadet	moos-kah-day	Table	W	D	CCC
Muscatel	mus-kah-tel	Fortified	Gold	S	C
O					
Orvieto	orv-YEHT-oh	Table	W	D or Semi-S	CCC
Ouzo	OO-zoh	Liqueur	Cloudy W	S, licorice	CCC
P					
Pinot Blanc (Bianco)	pee-noh blahnc (bee-yahn-co)	Table	W	D	CCC
Pinot Grigio	pee-noh gre-dzho	Table	W	D	CCC
Pinot Noir	pee-noh nwahr	Table	R	D	C
Port(o)		Fortified	R	S	C
Puligny-Montrachet	poo-lee-nyee-mohn-ray-shey	Table	W	D	CCC
R					
Riesling	REES-ling	Table	W	D or S	CCC
Rioja	ree-OH-hah	Table	W or R	D	C or CCC

166 FOR MEN ONLY

Name	Pronunciation	Type	Color	Taste	Serving Temp.
S					
*Saké	SAH-kee	Rice beer	W	D, F	100°
*Sauterne	soh-tehrn	Table	W	D	CCC
Sauternes	soh-tehrn	Table	W	S	CCC
Sauvignon Blanc	soh-vee-nyohn blahn	Table	W	D or S	C
*Sémillon	seh-mee-yoh(n)	Table	W	D or S	CCC
Sherry		Fortified	Amber	D to S	C or CC
Soave	suah-vey	Table	W	D	CCC
*Sparkling Burgundy		Sparkling	W or R	Med. S	CCC
*Sylvaner	zil-vah-neh	Table	W	M/D	CCC
V					
*Vino Santo	vee-noh SANto	Table	W	S	CCC
Viognier	vee-on-nyeh	Table	W	S	CCC
Vouvray	voo-vreh	Table	W	M or S	CCC
Z					
Zinfandel	TZIN-fan-del	Table	R	D	C

APPENDIX D 167

APPENDIX E
MENU GUIDE

Question. What is a person called who speaks many languages? Answer: multilingual. What is a person called who speaks only one language? Answer: an American. Europeans have no difficulty hopping from country to country, and understanding the language and the restaurant menus of their neighboring cultures. An increasing number of fine restaurants in the United States cater to travelers and upscale patrons by printing their dishes in the language of origin, with an English translation underneath.

I had the good fortune to be born into an Italian family **and** in New York, where my family had not only the benefit of the tastes and aromas of great home cooking, but learned to be comfortable dining in excellent restaurants representing a cornucopia of cuisines, or asking for *knishes* and *kielbasa*. I took it all for granted. I also had the foresight to study French, because I believed it to be the language of sophisticated people.

You too, will appear sophisticated when you don't have to ask what basic dishes are on the menu. You don't want to look like a rookie. To be world-class, recognize and use properly the names of often-ordered foods and dishes—that's part of your game plan.

Foods are listed according to course sequence in alphabetical order, accompanied by the American name.

ITALIAN

Antipasti – Appetizers

Bruschetta: Roasted bread rubbed with garlic, dribbled with olive oil, and seasoned with salt and pepper

Carpaccio: Paper thin slices of raw beef, seasoned with olive oil, lemon, basil, salt and pepper

Crostini: Halved slices of bread topped with sliced fresh tomatoes, mozzarella, anchovy, ham, etc. and toasted in the oven

Grissino: Bread sticks

Prosciutto e fichi: Figs wrapped in smoked ham

Zuppa – Soup

Brodo: Broth
Minestrone: Hearty vegetable soup
Stracciatella: Eggdrop soup
Zuppa di scarola e riso: Escarole and rice soup
Zuppa di vongole: Clam soup

Pasta

Cannelloni: A large tubes filled with meat, cheeses and spinach, and baked in a sauce

Capelli d'angelo: Angel hair

Cappelletti: Small domes filled with meat or cheese

Fettuccine: Flat noodle, wider than linguine

Fusilli: Corkscrews

Gnocchi: Small dumplings made of potatoes or flour

Lasagna: Two-inch wide flat noodles, layered with red sauce, meat and cheeses

Linguine: Flat type of spaghetti

Macaroni: General name for all commercially-made dried pasta

Manicotti: Large tubes filled with cheees and baked in sauce

Maruzze: Seashells

Penne: Pens

Ravioli: Two-inch squares encasing meat, cheese or spinach

Rigatoni: Large pasta tubes, often used in baked dishes

Spaghetti: Long, thin strands of pasta

Tagliatelle: Classic egg noodle, about three-fourth-inch wide

Tortellini: Small, ring-shaped dumplings

Ziti: Medium-sized ribbed tubes, often used in baked dishes

Salsa – Sauces

Al burro: With butter
Alla carbonara: With browned bacon, egg yolks, Parmesan cheese and cream
Marinara: Meatless tomato sauce with onions, garlic and spices
Pesto: Blended or mortar ground basil leaves, olive oil, pine nuts, and garlic
Piccata: Sharp or spicy with lemon, butter

Fruitti di Mare e Pesce – Seafood and Fish

Acciughe: Anchovies
Aragosta: Lobster
Calamari: Squid
Cozze: Mussels
Filetto di sogliole: Fillet of sole
Gamberi: Shrimp
Pescespada: Swordfish
Scampi: Large shrimp
Scungilli: Conch
Soglia: Sole
Tonno: Tuna
Vongole: Clams

Pollo – Poultry

Cacciagione: Game
Cappone: Capon
Pollo: Chicken
Pollo alla cacciatore: Seasoned fried chicken with anchovy, olives, capers and tomato paste
Taccino: Turkey

Carne – Meats

Agnello: Lamb
Bistecca: Steak
Braciola: Beef filet, wrapped around a combination of various fillings
Coppa: Large pork sausage
Fegato: Liver
Maiale: Pork
Manzo: Beef
Mortadella: Sliced pork cut for sandwiches
Pancetta: Bacon
Polpette: Meat balls
Salsiccia: Pork sausage
Scaloppine: Quarter-inch-thick slices breaded and sautéed veal
Vitello: Veal

Contorni – Vegetables

Carciofi: Artichokes

Ceci: Chickpeas

Funghi: Mushrooms

Melanzana alla Parmigiana: Baked eggplant with Parmesan cheese

Patate: Potatoes

Piselli: Green peas

Polenta: A thick porridge made from corn

Porcini: Wild mushrooms

Riso: Rice

Risotto: A dish of rice stir-cooked in simmering broth and usually served with cheese

Formaggio – Cheese

Asiago: A hard cheese with a nutty texture that is good for snacking

Bel Paese: A soft, creamy, slightly sweet cheese; pairs well with pears and apples and chardonnay wine

Fontina: A delicate semi-soft cheese with a nutty flavor

Gorgonzola: A soft, strong-flavored cheese with blue-green veining

Mascarpone: A mild, creamy cheese often served with fresh fruit

Mozzarella: A light-flavored cheese made from water buffalo milk

Parmigiana-Reggiano: A hard cheese, usually grated over a red sauce

Pecorino: Made with sheep's milk with a slightly sharp taste

Provolone: Delicate and mild when young, sharper when aged

Ricotta: A sweet, white cheese

Dolce – Desserts

Amaretto: Cookie made of almonds, sugar and egg white

Biscotti: Hard cookies with nuts

Cannoli: Pastry tube filled with blended ricotta, whipped cream, and chocolate bits

Cassata: A three-flavored filling of ricotta cheese, candied fruit and grated chocolate with sponge cake

Gelato: Ice cream

Granita: Fine-grained shaved ice and fruit syrup

Sorbetto: Sherbet

Tiramisu: A coffee- and cognac-soaked cake made with ladyfingers and mascarpone

Zabaglione: A soft, airy, and warmed dessert of egg yolk, sugar and Marsala

Frutta — Fruits

Ciliege: Cherries
Fragola: Strawberry
Limone: Lemon
Mela: Apple
Pesca: Peach
Pomodoro: Tomato
Uva: Grapes

Agguintia — Miscellaneous

Al dente: Cooked firm "to the teeth"
Al forno: Baked in the oven
Calzone: Wheels of dough filled with meats, cheese or vegetables, then folded in half, pinched closed, and baked
Crudo: Raw
Fritto: Fried
Frittata: Omelet
Insalada: Salad
Latte: Milk
Noci: Nuts
Pane: Bread
Pollo: Chicken
Uova: Eggs

FRENCH

Hors d'oeuvres – Appetizers

Crudités: Raw vegetables
Escargots: Snails
Fois gras: Minced spread of goose or duck liver

Potage – Soup

Bisque: A puree, served as thick soup
Bouillabaisse: Fish soup with leeks, tomatoes, fennel, garlic and onions
Cassoulet: A white bean stew
Consommé: Meat stock that has been enriched, concentrated, and clarified
Soup à l'oignon: Onion soup

Fruits de Mer et Poissons – Seafood and Fish

Anchois: Anchovy
Coquille: Scallops
Crevettes: Shrimp
Homard: Lobster
Saumon: Salmon

Viante et Volaille – Meat and Poultry

Agneau: Lamb
Assiette anglaise: Coldcut platter

Bifteck: Steak
Bœuf rôti: Roast beef
Canard: Duck
Côte de veau: Veal chop
Grenouilles: Frog legs
Jambon: Ham
Langue: Tongue
Lard: Bacon
Pot-au-feu: Boiled beef
Ragoût: Meat, chicken or fish stew
Saucisson: Sausage
Tournedos: Filet mignon

Sauces et Préparation – Sauces and Preparation

Amadine: Made with almonds
À l'anglaise: Cooked in stock
À point: Red meat cooked medium-done
Béarnaise: Egg-thickened butter sauce finished with tarragon
Bien cuit: Well-done red meat
Béchamel: White sauce of milk and onion, thickened with butter and flour
Bleu: Red meat cooked very rare
Brochette: Food cooked on a skewer
Brouillé: Scrambled

Encroûte: Encrusted in pastry

Florentine: Garnished with spinach

Hollandaise: Butter sauce with a dash of cayenne pepper

À la jardinière: Fresh vegetables served with stewed or braised meat and chicken

Lyonnaise: Prepared with onions

Mornay: Béchamel sauce mixed with cream and cheese

Saignant: Red meat cooked rare

Légumes et Fruits – Vegetables and Fruits

Ananas: Pineapple

Articahaut: Artichoke

Asperge: Asparagus

Aubergine: Eggplant

Avocat: Avocado

Cerise: Cherry

Campignon: Mushroom

Chous: Cabbage

Citron: Lemon

Epinards: Spinach

Fraise: Strawberry

Framboise: Raspberry

Frites: French fries

Haricots: Beans

Haricots verts: String beans

Pamplemousse: Grapefruit
Pommes: Apples
Pommes de terre: Potatoes

Fromage – Cheese

Beaufort: A hard cheese that is fragrant when young and more pungent as it ages.
Brie: A creamy cheese with a nutty flavor. It is a dessert cheese best served at room temperature.
Camembert: Has soft delicate, salty taste. This cheese goes well with a picnic lunch.
Compte: A hard cheese, similar to Gruyere. Serve with crackers, fruit, and French onion soup.
Münster: Different from domestic Münster cheese in that it has a strong flavor. Serve with beer and brown bread.
Roquefort: A blue mold cheese made from sheep's milk; it has a sharp taste. Eaten as a dessert cheese.
St. Paulin: A mild dessert cheese that goes well with fruit.

Désserts – Desserts

Baba au rhum: A cake with raisins soaked in rum syrup
Beignets de pommes: Apple fritters
Chantilly: Whipped cream flavored with vanilla
Charlotte russe: A small, molded sponge cake topped with Bavarian or Chantilly cream

Choux à la crème: Cream puffs

Coupe: Ice cream sundae

Crème bavoise: Bavarian cream

Crêpes confiture: Thin pancakes filled with jam or jelly

Éclair: Light pastry filled with whipped cream and spread with a chocolate glaze

Parfait glacé: Mixture of egg yolks, syrup and whipped cream

Divers – Miscellaneous

A part: Served separately

Bonne bouche: Literally, "good mouth." It is an after-dinner treat.

Carafe: A pitcher for the service of table wine

Carte du jour: Menu of the day

Déjeuner: Lunch

Desservir: Literally, "to clear the table."

Entrecôte: Sirloin steak

Entrements: A break, of either a side dish of food or entertainment, between courses.

Entrée: First course; in the United States sometimes called the main course

Hors d'oeuvres: Literally, "outside the main work." An appetizer served before the main meal.

Nouilles: Noodles

Pain: Bread

Paté de foie gras: Goose liver spread.

Table d'hôte: A full-course meal offering a limited number of choices and served at a fixed price to all guests in a hotel or restaurant.

APPENDIX F
TIPPING GUIDE

1: Recommended tip
0: Extra service only

DINING

1	**Wait staff:**	*15–20 percent**
0	**Maître d'hôte:**	*$5–$10 (occasionally and discreetly at a frequently used establishment)*
0	**Sommelier:**	*$3–$5 minimum or 8 percent of the wine bill given directly to the sommelier as you leave*
0	**Head wait staff:**	*same as maître d'hôte*
1	**Bartender:**	*15–20 percent*
1	**Buffet staff:**	*10 percent*
1	**Caterer:**	*15–20 percent of total bill*
1	**Checkroom attendant:**	*$.50 per item / $1 minimum*
0	**Musicians:**	*$1–$5*

* The tip is calculated on the bill *before* the tax is added. If service is not satisfactory, notify the management before the bill is paid. Custom varies based on the section of the country and luxury of the establishment, but in general give 20 percent for exceptional service, 15 percent for satisfactory service, 5–10 percent for poor service.

HOTELS

1	**Parking attendant:**	*$1 per retrieval*
1	**Baggage handler:**	*$1 minimum (car to lobby)*
1	**Bellhop:**	*$1 per bag carried to the room; $2 minimum per bag if heavy or oversized*
1	**Door attendant:**	*$1 per bag (car to lobby); $1–$5 to hail a cab, depending on the weather*
0	**Concierge:**	*$5–$10 per service*
1	**Room service:**	*15–20 percent*
1	**Room attendant:**	*$1 per person, per night, placed in an envelope*
1	**Housekeeper:**	*$1 per request*
0	**Washroom attendant:**	*$1 minimum*

TRAVEL

1	**Taxi driver:**	*5–20 percent*
1	**Parking valet:**	*$2 minimum*
1	**Limousine chauffeur:**	*15–20 percent*
0	**Shuttle driver:**	*$1 minimum*

1	Skycap:	*$1 per bag; $2 minimum per bag if heavy or oversized*
1	Train attendant:	*same as skycap*
1	Tour guide / driver:	*$2–$3 daily*

PERSONAL SERVICES

1	Hairdresser / colorist:	*15–20 percent**
1	Barber:	*15–20 percent*
1	Shampooer:	*$1–$2*
1	Manicurist:	*15–20 percent*
1	Masseuse / esthetician:	*5 percent*
	Electrologist:	*No tip***
	Personal trainer:	*No tip***
1	Shoe shine:	*$1 minimum*

* Generally, the proprietor of a business is not tipped.
** A gift or one week's fee at the holiday season.

CASINOS

0	**Showroom mâitre d'hôte:**	*$10–$20*
1	**Croupier / dealer:**	*one or two chips of winnings*
1	**Change person:**	*5 percent per jackpot*

CRUISE SHIPS

1	**Deck / Bar steward:**	*15–20 percent of bill*
1	**Dining steward:**	*$3–$5 daily*
1	**Cabin steward:**	*$3–$5 daily*

HOLIDAYS

1	**Babysitter:**	*An extra night's pay*
1	**Nanny / au pair:**	*One week's pay*
1	**Maid / butler / chauffeur:**	*One week's pay*
1	**Newspaper delivery:**	*$10–$15*
1	**Mail carrier:**	*Tips or gifts are prohibited*
1	**Resident door attendant:**	*$1–$100*
1	**Handyman / elevator operator:**	*$5–$15*
1	**Regular weekly delivery services:**	*$5–$10*
1	**Trash collector:**	*$5–$15 per person*
1	**Country club employees:**	*$100–$200 to the employee's holiday fund*

1   **Teacher:** *small gift*
1   **Private duty nurse:** *small gift*

MISCELLANEOUS

1	**Food delivery:**	*15 percent of the bill*
1	**Grocery delivery:**	*$1–$2*
0	**Movers / furniture delivery:**	*$5–$15*
0	**Fast-food server:**	*$.50–$1*
0	**Sporting-events usher:**	*$5–$10 (handed under the ticket to move to a better section in a half-full event)*
1	**Golf caddy:**	*5–20 percent of golf club charge*

OVERSEAS TIPPING

In Merrie Olde England, guests who wanted quick service dropped a coin in a cup situated at the front of each table in order *To Insure Promptness*. Today the TIP is left as a gratuity for prompt and courteous service the world over; but be careful because:

In France, *Servis Compris* means the tip has been included in the service. When traveling in Europe, if you do not see a gratuity charge posted on the check, ask the *maître d'hôte*.

In Germany, the change to the nearest euro is usually left as *Trinkgeld* when the service is included.

In Australia, China, Denmark, Finland, Iceland, and Japan, tipping is not customary.

In Europe, theater ushers are tipped the equivalent of a quarter, but not in England.

BIBLIOGRAPHY

Andries de Groot, Roy, and Esquire, Inc. *Esquire's Handbook for Hosts.* New York: Grosset & Dunlap, 1973

Baldridge, Letitia. *Guide to a Great Social Life.* Rawson Associates, 1987

Baldridge, Letitia. *Complete Guide to Executive Manners.* New York: Rawson Associates, 1993

Bridges, John. *How to Be a Gentleman.* Tennessee: Rutledge Hill Press, 2001

Dahmer, Sondra J. and Kurt W. Kahl. *The Waiter and Waitress Training Manual.* New York: John Wiley & Sons, Inc., 1996

Grossman, Harold J. *Grossman's Guide to Wines, Beers, and Spirits.* New York: John Wiley & Sons, 1983

Johnson-Bell, Linda. *Pairing Wine and Food.* New Jersey: Burford Books, 1999

Klinkenberg, Hilka. *At Ease...Professionally.* Chicago: Bonus Books, Inc., 1992

Meyer, Sylvia, Edy Schmid, and Christel Spühler. *Professional Table Service.* New York: John Wiley & Sons, 1991

Morgan, John. *Guide to Etiquette and Modern Manners.* Headline Book Publishing, 1996

Post, Peter. *Essential Manners for Men.* New York: HarperResource, 2003

Seldon, Philip. *Complete Idiot's Guide to Wine.* New York: Alpha Books of Simon & Schuster, 1996

Sichel, Peter M. and Judy Ley. *Which Wine?* New York: Peter M. Sichel and Judy Ley, 1975

Visser, Margaret. *Rituals of Dinner.* New York: Grove Weidenfeld, 1991

Von Drachenfels, Susanne. *Art of the Table.* New York: Simon & Schuster, 2000

INDEX

A
á la carte menu, 20
Agassi, André, 1

B
Bach, Johann Sebastian, 24
Beethoven, Ludwig van, 24
Bonaparte, Napoleon, 121
Borgnine, Ernest, 1
Brahms, Johannes, 24
broiled salmon steaks (recipe), 4, 6
business entertaining, 86–95
  hosting a business dinner at home, 95
  hosting a business luncheon, 87–95
  choreographing a meal, 87–88
  odd stuff (miscellaneous suggestions), 94–95
  paying the bill, 93–94
  seating arrangements, 89–91
  table rules and considerations, 91–93
  tipping, 93
  when to get down to business, 93
  working with the restaurant, 88–89
business luncheons and dinners as tests for competency, 70–71

C
candles, use of, 3, 13, 31, 133–134
caprese (tomato and mozzarella salad) (recipe), 4, 7–8
caterers and helpers, when to use, 53, 56, 95
champagne, 41, 51, 98, 112–113, 115, 121–122, 125, 127–128, 130–131, 136
Chesterfield, Lord (4th Earl of), 86
chilled strawberry soup (recipe), 8–9
chocolate mousse (recipe), 9, 11–12
cocktail parties, 57–58
  serving food, 57
  the bar, 57–58
coffee, 13, 25, 27, 43, 51–52, 60, 63, 66, 107–108
cooking advice, 29

D
dating advice, 1–2, 27

E
eating etiquette, 13–14
eating utensils, use of, 36–39, 47, 49–50, 52, 61–70, 72–85

1812 Overture (music), 23
ending the date, 27
entertaining a woman at home, 1–13
  decor, importance of, 2–3
  dinner menus and recipes, 4–12
  lighting ambience, 3
  music, types of, 3
  odd stuff (miscellaneous suggestions), 12–13
entertaining a woman in a restaurant, 13–23
  conversation, rules of, 22
  in the restaurant, 18–19
  making the reservation, 16–17
  odd stuff (miscellaneous suggestions), 18, 22
  ordering the food, 19–20
  ordering the wine, 21
  restaurant staff, 21–22
  the rules of engagement: dating and dining, 14–16
  what to wear, 17

F

filet mignon (recipe), 8–9
Franklin, Benjamin, 28
fried bananas flambé (recipe), 4, 8

H

herb butter (recipe), 9, 11
hosting a social dinner, 28–55

buffets, 56–57
defining the mess (dinner setting), 32–33
departure etiquette, 54
dishes and napkins, 33–36
  bread and butter plate, 35
  cover plate, 33
  cup and saucer, 35
  dinner plate, 34
  napkins, 35–36
  salad plate, 34
  soup plate, 33–34
glasses, 40–42
  for appetizer and dessert wines, 41
  for brandy, 42
  for light dinner wines, 41
  for red dinner wines, 42
  for water, 40
leading the conversation, 45
making the toast, 53–54
menu and music planning, 42–43, 58
odd stuff (miscellaneous suggestions), 54–56, 124–125
preparing invitations, 29–30
seating guests, 43–45
serving the dinner, 46–52
  cheeses, 49–50
  coffee, 51–52
  dessert course, 50–51
  fish course, 48

main meal: taste, 49
main meal: temperature, 49
main meal: texture, 49
main meal: tone, 48
odd stuff (miscellaneous suggestions), 52–53
salad course, 47–48
soup course, 47
setting the table, 31–32
place cards, 32
place settings, 31
silverware, 36–39
forks, 38
knives, 36–37
spoons, 39
starting the meal, 46
hosting tips, 28–29

J
Jet Propulsion Laboratory (La Cañada-Flintridge, CA), 4

K
KISS (Keep It Simple, Stupid) rule, 4

L
liquor and liqueurs, 42–43, 53, 55, 57–58, 114–116

M
male qualities that women complain about, 13–14
male qualities that women look for, 14, xvii
methods of obtaining these qualities, xvii–xviii
Martin, Judith, 15
Marty (film), 1
matching wines to food, 96–103
centrists' views, 97
neophytes' views, 97
odd stuff (miscellaneous suggestions), 102
traditionalists' views, 96–97
wine as an aperitif, 99
wines for appetizers, 99
wines for fish, 100
wines for hot and spicy foods, 102–103
wines for red meat, 101–102
wines for white meats, 101
Miss Manners. *See* Martin, Judith

O
order of wine service, 104–116
formal dining, 105–108
appetizer, 105
cheese, 107
chocolate, 107
coffee, 107
dessert, 107
fish, 106
fruit, 107
game, 106
meat, light, 106

    meat, red, 106
    poultry, 106
    salad, 106
    sorbet, 106
    soup, 105
  informal dining
    appetizer, 107
    coffee, 108
    dessert, 107
    general rules, 108
    main course, 107
out on the town, 23–26
  concerts, theater, opera and ballet, 24–26
    getting the tickets, 24
    theater manners, 24–26
  odd stuff (miscellaneous suggestions), 26

P

pasta (recipe), 9–11
pasta, types of, 12
patate alla trattoria (trattoria baked potatoes) (recipe), 4, 7
pepper mill, 4
place cards, use of, 32
prosciutto e fichi (Italian cured ham with figs) (recipe), 4–5

R

recipes, 4–12
restaurant etiquette, 13–14, 18–19, 21–22

S

Saintsbury, George, 40
salad tips, 12–13
shopping tips, 4, 12
Smith, Logan Pearsall, 59
sommelier (wine steward), 21
Stanhope, Philip Dormer. *See* Chesterfield, Lord (4th Earl of)
stracciatella (egg-drop soup) (recipe), 5–6

T

table and dining manners, 55–85
  courses of food, 61–66
    1st course: seafood cocktail, 61
    2nd course: soup, 61
    3rd course: fish, 62
    4th course: the entrée (main meal), 62
    5th course: salad, 62–63
    6th course: coffee and dessert, 63
    7th course: fruit, 64
  eating daunting foods, 70–83
    artichoke, 72
    asparagus, 72
    bacon, 72

beverages, 72–73
bread and rolls, 73
cake, 73
canapés, 73
candy, 73–74
caviar, 74
cheese, 74
chicken, turkey, duck and chops, 74–75
clams and mussels, 75
corn on the cob, 75
crackers, 75
doughnuts, 76
eggs, 76
fish, 76–77
fondue, 77
hors d'oeuvres, 77
lobster and crab, 77–78
odd stuff (miscellaneous suggestions), 84–85
olives, 78
oysters, 78
peas, 78–79
pizza, 79
salads, 79
sandwiches, 79
sauces, 79
shrimp cocktail, 75–76
snails, 80
soup, 80
spaghetti, 80
sushi, 81
eating fruit, 81–83
    apricots, nectarines, peaches and plums, 81
    bananas, 81
    cherries, 81
    figs, 82
    grapefruit, 82
    grapes, 82
    kumquats, 82
    mangos, 82–83
    melons, 83
    oranges and tangerines, 83
    papayas, 83
    pineapple, 83
finger bowl, 64–65
odd stuff (miscellaneous suggestions), 65–66
place setting, 60
styles of eating, 66–70
    American zigzag style of eating, 68–69
    European style of eating, 66–68
    odd stuff (miscellaneous suggestions), 70
table d'hote menu, 19
Tchaikovsky, Peter Ilyich, 23
tipping at a restaurant, rules of, 22, 93
types of wine
    after-dinner liqueurs, 114–116
        amaretto di sarronno, 115
        anisette, 114
        cherry Herring, 115

cointreau, 115
crème de cacao, 115
drambuie, 115
grand marnier, 115
Irish cream, 115
kahlúa and tia maria, 115
ouzo, 116
pernod, 116
aperitifs, 108–109
dessert wines, 113–114
red wines, 111–112
earthy, 111
fruity, 111
grassy, 111
nutty, 112
oaky, 112
vanilla, 112
rosés, 109
sparkling wines, 112–113
brut, 113
demi-sec, 113
doux, 113
extra-brut, 113
extra-sec, 113
sec, 113
white wines, 110

V
Visser, Margaret, xvii

W
Washington, George, 31
wine, 1, 4, 9, 21, 40–43, 47, 50–51, 53–56, 58, 60, 63, 96–136

wine bottles, 117–129
chilling wine, 130–131
odd stuff (making opened wine last), 131
decanting of
decanting methods, 133–134
definition, 132–133
number of servings at dinners or a party
champagne, 127–128
liqueurs or cordials, 128
with aperitifs, 127
with desserts, 128
with luncheons, 128
with multicourse meals, 128
with simple meals, 128
number of servings per bottle, 126–128
opening bottles of sparkling wine, 121–122
opening bottles of still wine, 119–121
using a single lever corkscrew, 120
using a spiral corkscrew, 119–120
pouring, 121, 125–126
aromatic drinks, 125
brandy, 126
champagne, 125
red wine, 125
white wine and rosé, 125

serving temperature of, 131–132
  serving wine at dinner
      formal service, 135
      informal service, 135–136
      odd stuff (miscellaneous
        suggestions), 136
  shapes of, 117–118
  storing wine
      light wine, 129
      red wine, 130
  the cork, 122–123
wine dyes and tannins, 98
wine in a restaurant
  approval of the wine, 124
  etiquette, 123–124
  tasting of the wine, 124

PROFESSIONAL PROFILE

Naomi Torre Poulson, founder of The Etiquette Company, presents Southern California's leading programs in business protocol and dining etiquette. Recognized as an expert in her field, Naomi provides corporate training, executive coaching, and consulting services. She teaches professionals the skills required to "outclass" the competition in personal polish, image, decorum and presentation. Naomi's professional credits include:

TELEVISION: for Bravo—*His and Hers*; The British Broadcasting Company, *Television 2*; CBS *Family Affair* ; Fox 6 *News Live*; London Broadcasting Company; KABC's *Eye on L.A.*; Fine Living Ultimate Gift Guide.

RADIO: ABC's *Sam Donaldson's Live in America*; CJAD *HOLDEROVERNIGHT* (Canada); the British Broadcasting Company's *Radio 5 Live Global*; London Broadcasting Company's *Tessa Dunlap Show*.

MAGAZINES AND NEWSPAPERS: *Forbes*; *Cosmopolitan Magazine*; *Orange Coast Magazine*; *Men's Health*; *Woman's Day*; *Wall Street Journal*; *Los Angeles Times*; *San Jose Mercury News*; *Orange County Register*; as well as numerous trade and business publications.

Naomi Poulson earned a bachelor's degree in liberal arts and holds an upper-division California education credential. She earned her master's degree in business management, and worked for NASA's Caltech/Jet Propulsion Laboratory for more than ten years. Naomi received her professional etiquette training in Washington, D.C. She holds the highest certification available as an Independent Corporate and International Protocol Consultant.

Contact Naomi

The author welcomes your questions and comments. Please address your remarks or requests for corporate seminars and group or individual coaching to: e-mail: enquiries@etiquette-school.com.

Please visit our website at www.theetiquettecompany.com or www.etiquette-school.com.